From Harvard to Hell and Back

By Eric H. Sigward

SECOND EDITION

Scribe Publishing, Philadelphia
www.scribenet.com

From Harvard to Hell and Back

An account of my life from 12 to 25 years of age

By Eric H. Sigward
1st edition, 1975
2nd edition, 2003

**To the memory of my mother
— Angela Maria Sigward**

CONTENTS

ACKNOWLEDGEMENTS

I am grateful to the following people for their contributions to this book. Thanks to James Hervey-Bathurst for the only photo I could obtain of Mudi Annelise Hellberg. Thanks to William Lord Huntingdon, William Hastings-Bass, for calling Mudi and reestablishing communication. Thanks to Judith Bruce for her photo. Thanks to the many editors: David Rech at Scribe in Philadelphia; Nacci Press in Allentown, Pennsylvania. Thanks to William R. Clinton, Dr. Howard D. Sharpe, and Ken Sandler for proofreading. Thanks to Robert Whitney for editing and rewriting suggestions. Robert is a representative of the first generation of Harry Parker's Harvard rowing dynasty and a Porcellian Club brother. His remarks, therefore, were invaluable. Thanks to Steve Brooks for spelling suggestions and for publishing my rowing articles.

Thanks to the people who encouraged me by their candid remarks: Alan Rogowsky, Harry Parker, Talal Debs, Tom Ireland, David Braga, Bayn Johnson and Ken Sandler. I grasped hold of their remarks like gold. Thanks to Ian and Josie Gardiner who were the first to say they loved the book.

Thanks to David Fuller for suggesting I use real names, and thanks to those who approved once they saw themselves in print: Joe Kanon, Mudi Annelise Hellberg, Linda Muller Vasu, Judith Bruce, and John McKinnon. I don't think I could have proceeded without their approval.

I) HORACE MANN SCHOOL FOR BOYS

CHAPTER 1: SCHOOL FOR BOYS

All times I have enjoyed
Greatly, have suffered greatly, both with those
That loved me and alone.
— Tennyson, *Ulysses*

Horace Mann, a selective private school in the Bronx, New York had six grades and a student body of about 600 boys to fill six grades. It now has twelve grades and is coeducational. It is situated atop a large hill at the end of the Broadway IRT line, across the road from Van Cortlandt Park. Although I did eventually go to Harvard, I was by no means the most talented Horace Manner. For instance, Ken Frisoff was the top scholar in all subjects from the first form. He edited three school publications, won a National Merit Scholarship, and went on to Phi Beta Kappa at Harvard. This school was a rigorous place.

The six years of study at HM were filled with sports, instruction, and thought. My ambitions motivated my efforts, for I desperately wanted to succeed, and the whole process of my early education was like preparing for a great crew race. Every day counted, every practice, every stroke. But one day I hoped to step into a delicately balanced racing shell and find that all my labors had been worthwhile. The initial drudgery of practice had resulted in a boat that fairly skimmed over the water like a huge swan in flight. In the same way, by day-to-day effort, I set about fulfilling the high school dream; and similarly one day I hoped the pieces would fit together and I would be enjoying a Harvard education.

When I entered HM that September at age 12 I had just left

my steady girlfriend of grammar school days, Linda Muller. We had exchanged identification bracelets two years earlier and had been steady companions over ice cream and Coke. She was a worthy object of any boy's love. Intellectually rugged at age 11, she could at that time read as well as most people four or five years older than herself. She was a true princess, schooled in etiquette, dress, and some ideas about the courtly way to conduct herself. We met at a birthday-party dance where by chance I picked her number out of a basket. I approached my little friend who was sitting in a large easy chair, her fierce Athenian-gray eyes flashing with love and war. You might think she was unique and after a fashion she was, but she was a twin! Ever and always, her slightly younger sister, Susan, was in tow and her perfect mirror image.

We danced to tunes like *At the Hop, Kisses Sweeter than Wine* and *The Purple People Eater*, and afterwards went to *Schraft's* on 79th Street for ice cream. I'm afraid I was a tearful and emotional lover demanding absolute loyalty and psychological support from her.

I have mentioned this phase of my life for two reasons. First, Linda followed me in person and in dream, like the ghost of a lost lover one always wishes to please, from the third grade until I graduated from Cambridge University sixteen years later. And she appeared and exited at several important junctures in my life.

Secondly, I want to explain that when I entered HM in 1958 I knew beyond doubt who would be my heroine, the impossible dream for whom I would fight, long, and perish.

Given a woman to fight for, there were several other goals about which I was certain at age twelve. At that time there was a black student in school named Stan Thomas, perhaps the most spectacular athlete and leader in HM's history. He captained the three big teams: football, basketball, and baseball; and did broad jumping events on the side. His flashing runs on the gridiron had astounded the city for three years. Evidence of his popularity and natural leadership ability was his chairing of the community council, the student government, and leading his class as president for four years. A true hero, he had the special grace of being athletic and gentlemanly. I set my goal to be like Stan — scholar, athlete, and leader. In addition, I wanted to go to Harvard, and have Linda in that undefined adolescent way.

I think Horace Mann encouraged an aggressive spirit because by the time I was in the second form (age 13) I noticed that Andy Tobias had a Harvard loose-leaf binder. His vision had been determined fairly early in his career, too. And eventually he did go up to Harvard.

It is certainly wrong to strive towards heroism for its own sake, because one loses love of life in the process. To fall in love with the image of success is to lose love for the activity. I was as guilty as the next man for loving glory rather than football, honors rather than knowledge. Yet I was opening in new ways at HM. Before HM I had done little reading; now the subject I studied first and longest was English. It is here that I have found a spontaneous and compulsive love. I delighted in ancient mythology, epic, drama, and romantic poetry. My favorite works were *The Odyssey*, *Moby Dick*, *Crime and Punishment*, and several of Shakespeare's plays.

Mathematics carried with it the joy of building. Problems could be solved in balanced, orderly fashion. We are fascinated by the logic of questions like this: if Bob has twice as many apples as Hal and three fewer than Mike who has thirteen, how many apples do Bob and Hal have? These kinds of questions attract us with their clarity and their promise of sure answers.

The sciences we studied presented us with the broad and often mysterious vistas of creation. Each science revealed a special depth and complexity of nature. Haven't volcanoes always intrigued us — the thought of vast subterranean seas of molten lava and thundering mountains that in an instant can explode, creating whole islands of mountains? Who has not wondered at the growth of a fetus and eventually a whole human being from a single impregnated cell? What are the forces that hold together the atom and the galaxy? These are the matters we studied in earth science, biology, chemistry, and physics. I am admittedly only a dilettante in these things, but this does not remove the thrill of learning some new fact of nature. The many hours I spent in labor over science courses did not produce in me a great skill, but I grew to appreciate that ability in others; and I can certainly understand the ongoing passion of the true scientist.

In the six years of my school career I took American, ancient and modern european history. While European and American history have not yet fully captured my interest, ancient history has always drawn me with its clear, clean, sunbaked romance. Babylon, Israel, Egypt, Greece, Rome — religion, law, architecture, literature, government — these civilizations and their contributions leap at us from the pages of history. We are amazed at how so few people could produce as many and as great original works as they did. For centuries in modern times men have returned to the old places to admire the artifacts that belong to the glory of the ancient world. I relished the study of Latin and Greek, and I can remember the awe with which I first beheld the Coliseum in Rome the summer of 1968. I thought, "My mother taught me about the Coliseum years ago." As I viewed the crumbling walls of the old structure, now surrounded by traffic and pedestrians, I recollected scenes of gladiatorial spectacles and Christian persecutions.

Of all subjects, languages have always come easiest. I'm sure that this is because I grew up in a trilingual family, my mother speaking Italian and my father German in addition to English. Contrary to the warnings of many classmates, I fully enjoyed Caesar's *The Gallic Wars* and Virgil's *Aeneid*. The centurion who though badly wounded fought on for Caesar while leaning on his shield thrilled me. Nor can one forget Virgil's great insight that a war was started in part because of the fury of a woman whose beauty had been scorned. The Spanish I acquired at HM has stood me in good stead; I have found occasion to use it in New York as well as on trips to Spain and Mexico.

As I have already mentioned, Horace Mann was rigorous and I was not a distinguished scholar but rather a competent and earnest one. There were many of my peers who had fathomed life and letters deeper than I. However, given that I was a "jock" and that my grades placed me at the uppermost quintile of the class, Harvard was certainly within reach.

The treatment of students by teachers was fatherly and benevolent. When we entered HM we learned that you had to wear a jacket and tie to school – no sneakers, and whites to gym. And you called your teachers "Sir." Mr. Reilly, a teacher of several language courses, required that we bring a comb, nail file, and handkerchief to class. And for inexcusable stupidities, like leaving your briefcase in the aisle "to try and trip me," we were playfully beaten on the rear with a blackthorn stick to the instructive count of a foreign language. Mr. Metcalf stoned students with a tennis ball if he caught them napping in his Latin class. If a momentarily stymied student should ask, "What does this word mean, sir?" he was met with Mr. Metcalf's reply, "Why should I tell you? It took me ninety years to learn it." On one class day, Mr. Metcalf told my mother, "You have a fine son, but I can tell it's all from his father's side." Then he went to my father and told him the reverse: all my good qualities were from my mother's side. Mr. Oliver told us: "You speak French like a cow."

"Vous parlez français comme une vache espagnole."

Mr. Quinn's football talks were classics in diatribe: "Quijano, do you need a net? That pass only hit you in the chest, catch the ball! Hliddal, you make me want to puke. Look at the size of you; you could have wrapped that guy up and put him in your back pocket, but no, you're la-dee-dahing down the field like a prima donna. You are something else."

My friendship with Mr. Clinton has covered many years since I was a junior at HM. He is a teacher who delights and encourages many students each year, both in class and on his own time outside of class. One of his classes might take this form: the door swings open at once as if for a dramatic entrance, and in walks Mr. Clinton. Several students are following him in train, for here is a man who commands a court, a retinue or a round table. Mr.

Clinton's blue eyes are large and commanding – not by terror so much as by sensitivity, martyrdom, and grace. He rules by tradition, by election, and by suffering. One sweep of the comb has neatly parted his gray locks, and a Brooks Brothers tweed jacket covers his generous body. He looks much like a young and buoyant Charles Laughton, full of talent and intelligence.

Immediately, 30 sixteen-year-olds rise from their chairs in the modern European history class. And thus Mr. Clinton begins:

"Apfel, stand up, who said you were special?"

Apfel gets up out of his seat with one of those indifferent, sad expressions on the side of his mouth as if to say, "I am different and I need special attention."

Mr. Clinton hasn't finished his complaint: "Take your hands out of your pockets. Scratch on your own time. Take that expression off your face before I hit you. Don't push me, Apfel, you know I'll do it. And don't ever come into my class with those tight pants on. You can put them back on when you're on Broadway."

At this, the class breaks up laughing and Apfel is feeling warmer. "Be seated, all right Apfel, since you're setting the rules here, tell us about the provision of the Treaty of Versailles concerning the production of champagne."

"It was restricted to the Champagne district of France and forbidden in the other European countries, though Italy produced something like champagne and called it sparkling wine."

"Very good, Apfel. See me after class." That afternoon Apfel will discuss his family life and college goals with Mr. Clinton. There will be a warm handshake, and Mr. Clinton will look into Apfel's eyes with an expression that says, "You now know me, you are my friend."

Mr. Clinton and I have talked delightedly for hours — on the roof of Tillinghast Hall as spring brought up the first grass, on Four Acres overlooking the campus and on Broadway next to the elevated train. The teachers at Horace Mann were among the most dedicated and competent men I have known. Horace Mann is by any standard a fine school and I have received from her a love for knowledge and good work.

My father had been an intercollegiate boxing champion in Germany, and later became a physical director. After arriving in America he opened a private gymnasium on 54th Street in downtown Manhattan. There he provided lessons in boxing, judo, jiu-jitsu, karate, and weight-lifting, along with massage and steam bath for New York businessmen. Therefore, my development as an athlete was an inheritance. By age twelve I had swum across the Hudson River several times at summer camp. And one-by-one I had acquired sports: roller skating, ice skating, tennis, swimming, horseback riding, and hiking. In high school I earned letters in football, swimming, wrestling, baseball, and track; and at Harvard I rowed.

When I entered HM in 1958 I was already one of the better swimmers in my class, but my overall condition was flabby. Consequently, I went into a remedial physical fitness class. Within two years I was crashing through the line for long yardage, and sports had become the real passion of my high school career. Sure I liked to study, but how could a book ever compare with the real sweat and glory of sport? Could classroom intellectualism compare with the profound friendships one develops with team-mates or with one's coach? One could read history, but on the football field or in the pool, history and art were in the *making*. The grace or agility only sniffed in language or literature were seen and felt on the wrestling mat or track. Nothing could compare with the thrill of a touchdown run, a good block, or the coach's praise.

On the football field I presumed that each man took life into his own hands, and I did everything I could to convince the opposing team of this. I would hit hard at the throat when throwing blocks, or tackle high around the neck if I could get the angle. In one game I missed blocking a pass which resulted in a touchdown for the other team. I was weeping with fury as we lined up to receive the kick-off. The ball was kicked and I ran down the field as blocking-protection for the ball carrier. My assigned man was standing flat-footed, waiting for us to come down to him. Taking advantage of his hesitation, I put down my head and hit him hard under the chin at full gallop with my helmet. His feet lifted off the ground and he sailed six feet off the field and landed unconscious on the sidelines. I stood a bit dazed from the blow and waited as coaches and trainers checked his condition. His first words on regaining consciousness were, "Don't send me back in there."

The winter of my junior year the dreadful occurred. My left shoulder was wrenched from its socket during wrestling practice. Besides wrestling, my swimming career was also ended because the shoulder continued to dislocate on gliding turns. And when fall of senior year arrived, although I was captain of the team and in the best shape of my career, my shoulder would not stand up to the tugging and shocking of football.

Dumbfounded by this awful stroke of luck, I tried again and again to overcome the injury. For six weeks I lived and slept with my arm in a sling, hoping that I would once again feel nylon pants and guards on my thighs, shoulder pads on my chest. My father called our headmaster — could I play? I just couldn't be kept out that season. But for all my patience and wit, the shoulder would not stay in place. The first play of my first game I threw a block, landed with my arms out-stretched and my shoulder popped. I ran to the sidelines with my broken wing, knowing instinctively that one gray shadow had drifted over my youth. I sat out what I had anticipated would be the best season of my career. There followed a long period of impotent bitterness when I tried to fathom the cause for this wound. Why had it happened to me? Who had done it? Only unanswerable questions.

Another element of my high school dream materialized junior year. Several teachers suggested that I was a likely candidate for the highest offices in the school. On the one hand, I could run for chairmanship of the community council; on the other hand, I could be editor of the yearbook, a valid publishing assignment. My head expanded for an instant as I saw that I was guaranteed at least one of the top offices. If I lost the election for the council, I could still edit the yearbook. Harvard was close at hand, I thought. The joyful thrill of being close to the goal filled my brain. My grades were good, athletics good, and now a new increment to the resume: leadership.

I chose the council over the yearbook and won office by a good margin. My job for the coming year would be to lead the school within the framework of the student government. In the next year we discussed and voted on such issues as school rules, relationships with neighboring schools and the structure and function of committees.

In the autumn before entering Harvard, I visited Cambridge with Ken Frisoff and two other friends. Myron Miller, an ex-Horace Manner, entertained us in his rooms at Thayer Hall. At one point our two friends went into an adjoining suite leaving Ken, Myron, and me in the same room. "Well, who's going to make it to Harvard next year," I asked. Myron replied, "I assume that everyone in this room will be here next year." Ken and I looked at one another and back to Myron. Yes, we two would make it. The others would have to go someplace else, maybe Yale or Chicago. The four of us regrouped, though now there was a stern truth among us: some are chosen, some are not. We put on coats and walked out into the Yard. Turning the corner of Thayer Hall we entered the inner Yard. It was a crisp fall evening, and dormitory lights looked like sparkling crystal. Before us sat the immensity of Widener Library in full, illumined glory. I felt like Bunyon's Pilgrim whose burdens dropped as he faced the splendrous gates of Heaven.

"The pillars are decorative but not functional," Myron quipped. "They don't really hold up the roof, rather they're hung from it. Silly, architecturally."

A further conviction that there was a special Harvard identity emerged as I waited tables at Howard Johnson's in Greenwich Village the summer before school started.

"You're a good waiter, kid. Where do you go to school?" one

customer asked.

"Harvard," I replied.

"No, you don't."

"Yes I do."

"No, you don't, *no one* goes to Harvard."

"O.K.," I conceded, "I don't go to Harvard, you're right. I go to Alfred."

"How do you like Alfred?"

"Just fine."

"What do you take there?"

"Ceramics."

"That's interesting."

For him the name of Harvard was a myth and a fiction that had to be maintained. He simply refused to believe that anyone actually went there.

In the way of extracurricular activities, there were two that brought me much satisfaction. Until age 14, I was a Boy Scout, ultimately achieving Eagle rank. The activities of scouting include some of the best tastes of reality. Camping, crafts, teamwork and life in the out-of-doors are the solid elements of the Boy Scout experience. Can anyone deny the fresh feeling of hiking through a forest, over an icy lake, or up a prehistoric ravine? How much better can one feel than when cooking over an open fire or wielding a two-handed axe? The knowledge and experiences of Scouting continue to carry me to the good places on earth.

A second fortunate activity of those days was summer camp. Because my father had been a friend of Coach "Moose" Miller, I was invited to his Camp Moosilauke in Orford, New Hampshire, for summers. My body grew hard and brown on New Hampshire rivers and mountains, and I was free to read and talk with campers and counselors.

At Horace Mann I had several girlfriends in the upper grades with whom I danced and dated. I could not quite explain either to myself or to my parents or teachers what I needed in the way of love or sex, and so those imponderables became part of the lonely, secret road of adolescence. I hope the subsequent account will clarify these issues, though I cannot begin to presume authority in this area. Late in my senior year I met Linda Muller again at a model United Nations conference, and feeling confident in my many accomplishments, struck up a relationship with her again. At 18 she had grown into a strong and winsome woman, still fiercely beautiful. We dated several times, and in the next year she went to Wellesley, only 14 miles from Harvard. Now all the pieces of the puzzle were falling into place, even my long lost and almost forgotten Linda.

When I graduated from Horace Mann I had achieved the goal envisioned six years earlier. Honors conferred for my work included membership in the *Cum Laude* Society for scholars, the Varsity Club for athletes, and the Archon Society for leaders. In addition, I was awarded medallions for work in Spanish and Latin. Although I never got to play football senior year, within the season I had what I coveted most. I received notice of my acceptance by Harvard with an offer for scholarship aid. There remained only the formalities of finishing the year before going, so to speak, to Heaven.

II) HARVARD UNIVERSITY

CHAPTER 2: COLLEGE FRESHMAN

In Xanadu did Kubla Khan
A stately pleasure-dome decree:
Where Alph, the sacred river, ran
Through caverns measureless to man
Down to a sunless sea.
    – Coleridge, *Kubla Khan; Or a Vision in a Dream*

One September afternoon I mounted my bike in front of Greenough Hall, then cycled up Massachusetts Avenue towards the Coop. I took a left onto Boylston, pedaled hard for a short block, and cruised down towards the river. Up on the left I glanced to see the Georgian red brick and white wood of Eliot House. At Memorial Drive that runs along the Charles River I stopped to wait for the light and when it had changed, I headed for the opposite sidewalk, hopped the curb and rode to the edge of the river. Across the river lay Newell Boathouse, home of the Harvard crew, looking like a setting by Edgar Alan Poe, with a complex Victorian architecture of towers, porches, gables, and ramps. To the left and right ran the Charles, black and gold in the September dusk. Behind me rose the stately houses of Harvard, like mansions of Babylon. "Well, this is it," I thought, "You've made it."

On those banks I would play, dance, and love for the next four years; and by the time of my graduation in 1968, the youth generation would have had a spontaneous "happening" on the same shores. On the windy Charles waters I would tune my body into a taut rowing muscle. I got back on my bicycle and rode to dinner.

Freshmen in 1964 ate in the Union Dining Hall surrounded by

Teddy Roosevelt's hunting trophies. At dinner one might hear the names and thoughts of Ibsen, Shaw, T. S. Eliot, Arnold, or Keats. Our minds skipped to the boundaries of understanding. Amid the laughter and voices one might hear the loud clangor of tinkling glasses. Danny Boggs had just entered Hall with a beautiful Radcliffe girl, and the entrance was being heralded on all sides. Tales of intellectual splendor would daily exceed one another. Peter Nurkse had accepted sophomore standing, Joe Kanon was busy with his first novel, and Carl Saunders had built a still from chem lab equipment and was producing whiskey from apple juice in a shower stall. In a flash, my HM credentials were typical. Momentarily it became passe to reveal you were class president or captain of the football team. Brilliance and eccentricity abounded, and often the least likely proved to be the most talented. An unkempt R.O.T.C. man was superb at calculus, a debonair socialite had no equal in classics, and that foolishly intense next-door neighbor did chemistry in his sleep.

Having been thrown into Harvard's cauldron of fiery intellects, I was determined to be everything of a man I could. To carve my niche at Harvard I thought I must grow my hair long, drink deeply and become socially urbane. I had an intense desire to succeed along those lines as well as in my studies and in rowing. One evening I had an opportunity to drive a 50-cc Honda outside of my dorm. I handled the bike awkwardly and didn't even know that gears existed, but I took to it. Within a month I had acquired a driver's license and a 1959 250-cc Triumph Tigercub that was mostly in the shop. Its greatest claim to fame was that it froze stiff one cold night at Wellesley while I was visiting Linda. I kicked the starter pedal until frozen drops of sweat dotted the gas tank. Finally, I pushed the bike into an all night Laundromat and warmed it by an open dryer. When it started, I drove out the door and down the block, back home to the college.

Early in the spring when March winds were still sharp over the Charles, I traded the little blue bike for a red Norton Dominator, 600-cc with full racing gear. The set-back footpegs and low handlebars stretched one out over the bike to eliminate wind resistance. It accelerated so rapidly that riding in close traffic was hazardous because a touch of the throttle jumped you yards-at-a-time.

My academic work was initially poor. The release of tensions from high school had left me drifting without purpose at Harvard. And it was instantly evident that sloppy work failed to impress teachers. My first three grades were two C-'s and a D+ in calculus, English composition and government, respectively. In calculus I was both befuddled by the subject and surprised that it came so easily to other men in the class. I'm afraid that I still haven't fathomed the nature of my ignorance concerning government. Certainly I worked as hard for that subject as any but was unable to convince the professor of any skill. Nevertheless, despite this poor beginning, I was committed as ever to good grades and by the end of that year, I had pulled my average up to a Dean's List B.

Harvard, founded in 1636, is the oldest college in America. It had its origins as the first school for clergy in the new colonies but most Harvard people treat this fact like primate anthropology: "Of course we come from the apes, but thank goodness we're not like that anymore."

The freshman dormitories are situated in a quad called the Harvard Yard, and some of these houses served as quarters for George Washington's troops during the Revolution. Looking at the glowing lamps of Wigglesworth Hall I often imagined Washington's men bivouacked there for a cold Massachusetts winter.

There were many sides to Harvard — a center for study of the Italian Renaissance in Italy, a forest in New York State, and 16 professional schools. There was the unique Harvard style, tradition, point-of-view, or accent. The feeling that before all else, *Harvard was there,* epitomized it; and when all else had failed, Harvard would remain. Legend has it that a guest came to visit the President of Harvard and was told, "The President is in Washington seeing Mr. Taft." To the Harvard community, "The President" refers to its own, not the country's.

Three centuries of architecture commingle on the Harvard campus. Harvard Hall is puritan red brick and tile roofed. Memorial Hall is Victorian and gothic. The upperclassmen's houses are mock Georgian in red brick with white roofs and bell towers. And there are ultra-modern pieces by Pei, Corbusier and Frank Lloyd Wright. The Harvard library system with 14,500,000 volumes is the largest university library in the world. In the way of museums, the Fogg contains Chinese, Italian and French art. The Busch-Reisinger is devoted to Scandinavian and Germanic art, while the Peabody contains archaeological exhibits and famed glass flowers.

It is grandly apparent to the college freshman that this great mass of history, tradition, and material is for him. He is serene as the definite center of so much attention. We comfortably relaxed our stocking feet on the library tables, slept in desk stalls, and had snowball fights on the steps of the almighty Widener. Peabody's glass flowers were for girlfriends, Wordsworth's spreading chestnut tree was the site of a student coffeehouse, and the one-to-six student-faculty ratio meant careful instruction. It was not uncommon even for a freshman to have a Nobel Prize-winner, like George Wald in Biology, for a teacher.

Only freshmen lived in the yard. All of the upperclassmen were accommodated by the houses, 13 of them, which were small colleges within the larger university. Each was a self-contained community of about 350 students. An upperclassman lived, ate, worked, and was tutored in his house. Extracurricular activities like crew cut across house lines, and most instruction was given outside the houses in classrooms and laboratories. As upperclassmen, four of us lived in a suite of four bedrooms, two living rooms with fireplaces, and two bathrooms.

Radcliffe, founded in 1879, is filled with Harvard's coequals of the opposite sex. The Cliffies participated with Harvard men in all classroom work and received Harvard degrees.

I am the son of immigrants on both sides of my family. My father, as previously mentioned, hailed from Germany. My mother is a second-generation American from a Sicilian family. And so my parents were proud of a son who was now enrolled in one of America's elite social and intellectual institutions. My maternal grandfather, looking like a Roman senator with white hair, would sternly say to me, "Good, I'm proud of you: the more education, the better."

I came to Harvard with romantic preconceptions that had been encouraged by several experiences. A friend gave me Richard Bissell's *You Can Always Tell a Harvard Man*. Apparently all Harvard had to do to exist was hold a few luncheons among a few businessmen and millions of dollars flowed into Harvard coffers. Mr. Clinton had fed me on Harvard legends — how Kitridge, the Shakespearean scholar, had taught his classes with divine condescension. This was also the Kennedy era. Washington D.C. had become an annex for Harvard with men like Arthur Schlessinger, Jr., McGeorge Bundy, Robert MacNamara and others besides the three Kennedy brothers. A year earlier at the assassination of Jack Kennedy a freshman was seen weeping in the Yard, banging his head against one of the elms.

In the 1970's I met with varying responses to my Harvard career. A tourist in Madrid was indignant because Harvard had rejected his son. The college represented unfair social and academic discrimination. A carpenter in California surprised me one day with the information that he was actively following a debate between Harvey Cox and Buckminster Fuller, two Harvard professors. When I told him that I had gone there, he asked in an Alabama drawl, "Well, what are you doing here?" meaning at work as a carpenter. "Man, if I had that Harvard diploma I'd sit back and let the world make me a living. I'd be free!" For him Harvard was a ticket to bliss.

Some children grow up with musical ability, others will be philosophers, some will be poets and some will be carpenters. God's gift to me for pleasure and for employment has been an ability to perform logical functions and to group thoughts into concepts. Combined with the ability to appreciate cold logic, I have always had a thirst for that which tasted of myth and heroism. Tennyson's *Ulysses* has frequently spoken to my romantic wanderlust. "To sail beyond the sunset, and the baths / Of all the western stars, until I die." Recognizing this dual tendency towards both reason and romance, I thought that the social sciences, medicine and literature would be the best fields of concentration.

My first humanities class we read a perplexing author, C. S. Lewis. In both *Miracles* and *Screwtape Letters* Lewis dealt with issues which were at best irrelevant to me and at worst repugnant. In *Miracles,* Lewis proved the logical necessity for a belief in the supernatural. He argued that there are two basic views towards the created universe: the natural and the supernatural view.[1] The Naturalist believes that the universe is a closed system, that nature is the whole show and that nothing else exists. He sees it as a pond of infinite depth where there is nothing but water. The supernaturalist believes that in addition to nature, there is a supernatural being or world that exists outside of time and space and has produced nature. The pond is not merely water but has a bottom and earth under that.

If Naturalism is true, then there is no supernature to cause miracles. But Naturalism cuts its own throat because it contains a great self-contradiction. Because naturalism assumes that the rational mind is a part of nature, that makes it irrational. If the human mind must be grouped along with the other irrational events of nature then the validity of all thought is challenged. A man-made theory that makes the human mind irrational must itself be irrational. This is nonsense. It is as if someone stood up and solemnly declared, "There is no truth."

If there is no truth, then that statement is nonsense. Or if someone warned you on your first day at a new job, "Don't trust anyone in this office," would you trust him? When the validity of thought is undermined, everything becomes nonsense. Thus Lewis showed that reason could not be produced by nature. Supernaturalism, on the other hand, allows for reason that exists apart from nature but also penetrates it.

Conscience, likewise, cannot be a product of nature for there can never be absolute moral imperatives in nature, only situational ethics. But situational ethics are no ethics at all. True conscience in man is derived from a higher Moral Wisdom that exists absolutely and does not arise out of blind nature. Reason and morality are in fact miracles that pervade our daily mental operations. Given that these two operations of the human mind are not produced by nature and must come from a non-natural source, what might God look like if we saw him? Very much like Jesus Christ — full of grace and truth.

As a freshman, Lewis's arguments were utterly opaque to me. To begin with, I was not competent enough to follow his tightly woven logic. Nor did my background give me much appetite for beliefs of the orthodox kind. You may gather from my passion for sports, motorcycles, and romance that my mind was fixed on the true grit of a sensual life. I resented Lewis's insistence on belief in the supernatural as the basis for reason. I was a pushy kid from New York intent on success at Harvard. What did belief in the supernatural have to do with me?

Several years after reading Lewis I lost my hold on the rational world through the use of LSD. Drugs left me swimming on open seas of subjectivity and spiritualism. When I reread *Miracles* in 1971 and learned that simple faith in the validity of one's thinking was central to all other thoughts, I received a gift for which I am forever thankful. My mind has gratefully held onto this fact like an anchor in a storm. And I have since been able to rest on this realization in times of emotional and intellectual confusion.

Unfortunately, Lewis did not come into my life as a serious influence until after I had graduated from Cambridge University. Instead of solid logic, I filled my freshman mind with social sciences and behaviorist psychology for which Harvard is noted. Time does not permit a thorough discussion of behaviorism, but I think it is a naturalistic theory and so contains its own involuted poison.

There were geniuses good and bad at Harvard. One of the

better ones was Tom Ireland, my roommate for three years and friend since my first year at Horace Mann. He was terse and cryptic, and one always sensed that his words were deep waters filled with grave poetic significance. We had many enjoyable times together — often smoking pipes and talking until early hours, or riding our motorcycles through darkened Boston. He had a flare for genuine, delightful eccentricity — like buying a blowgun or postering his room with Schopenhauer quotations. His senior thesis on Joseph Conrad won a University prize as the best thesis in the Modern Languages Department. Characteristically, he promptly bet the prize money on horses, his current passion. The last I heard, he was living in a teepee on the plains of New Mexico with his new bride.

On the other side of the fence, it was often the case that as with Prince Hamlet, great intelligence was wasted. The successes many of us had known in classrooms produced fatal pride in our attitudes. We believed that we were little less than divine, self-sufficient, all knowing, without mother or father. At age 18 I had concluded that my parents had nothing more to teach me. I was set free in the world as a new star with none of the flaws I had observed in my parents. David Reissman, a Harvard sociologist, reflected on this childish romanticism as he recalled trying to explain the realities of life to a Cliffie. "I found it very difficult," he said, "to persuade a young woman of 18 to imagine what life would be like in later phases, even though her mother's experience and trajectory might have given her some perspective."

There was no lack at Harvard of the kind of love which the Greeks called *eros*, for every Saturday night buses and cars would form traffic jams into the Square, as college kids from all of Boston sought encounters at Harvard parties and dances. As a freshman, then, my eyes and heart were open to almost any kind of romantic tryst. As soon as I had arrived at Harvard I was dreaming of Radcliffe girls, Simmons girls, Wellesley girls and other college girls. I think that it is both humorous and mortifying that I was set free in the world like a rutting dog — humorous because sex is urgent even for proper Bostonians, but mortifying because I had no models of love or morality which I could emulate. The competitive instincts I had acquired at school, when applied to relationships, made me only an egotistical conqueror, not a loving human being. My girlfriends were often learning-experiments to be tried and abandoned.

Nevertheless, the bright glow of youth hung in the Harvard air; and many of the early moments as a freshman made profound and lasting impressions. A walk through the Square to meet friends; the Coop at Christmas filled with scarves, sweaters, books and Harvardnalia; Leavitt and Pearce Tobacco Shop with its rare pipes and old oars — these contributed to the delightful spirit of my new environment. But these experiences were not all wide-eyed tourism and romance. We played on the snowy steps of Widener Library like princes in a palace, but we also paid dues at its desks. This was no slothful or indolent play. We simply and continuously enjoyed apparent victory over life. Certainly I enjoyed Leavitt and Pearce, but I also read my daily rowing schedule in its window. Leavitt and Pearce became as common and enjoyable as lunch. I loved the frozen Charles — silent and austere in the snow. But there too I had earned oneness with the elements by hours of absorption while rowing.

If the success-motive characterized my high school career, my drive at Harvard was for identity. I wanted to be everything of a man I could and methodically pursued those activities that would give me a strong sense of self. Motorcycles, debauching, studying, rowing — in my early days I was emulating Marlon Brando — the "macho", the Wild One, the noble savage, Zorba, a berserker with poetry. Later I would more resemble Gatsby, affecting grace and fatal romanticism.

A resounding victory over Yale in crew, as number 5 in the first freshman boat, capped the year, heralding a brilliant future for our class in rowing. In addition, an exemplary essay in Social Sciences pulled grades up to the Dean's list. Half of the summer of '65 I again worked at Howard Johnson's in Greenwich Village, then drove cross-country with a friend, Frank Ritter, for the rest. That summer, while in New York, I kept company with a go-go dancer I met while driving the Norton Dominator on Madison Avenue.

CHAPTER 3: ROWING

It is the third commonness with light and air,
A curriculum, a vigor, a local abstraction . . .
Call it, once more, a river, an unnamed flowing,
Space-filled, reflecting the seasons, the folklore.
  – Wallace Stevens, *The River of Rivers in Connecticut*

When we first got on the water the fall of 1964, our freshman year, we were rowing in a cumbersome practice galley called "The Leviathan" that carried 16 men, eight on a side, and had an aisle up the middle for our coach. This was a far cry from the sleek eight-man racing shells we would one day row. And our style was commensurately poor. We did not dare use our legs at that stage for drive, nor did we feather the oar on the recovery. Just put in the blade of the oar; pull it through the water; draw it out at the finish. I would not have predicted that our class would see four golden years of Harvard rowing and eventually represent America at the 1968 Mexico City Olympics.

Our coach then was actually the varsity manager because our real coach was in Tokyo coxing an Olympic four-man shell, and would return to us as soon as the games were over. I was gleeful to learn that my coach was in the fabled Olympics; and in addition, had received a Phi Beta Kappa key at graduation for his work in English literature.

The boathouse looked like a castle — colossal, oaken, floodlit at night. It openly lay on the grassy banks of the Charles with a highway to the rear and the river in front. But perhaps because it rested somewhat beneath the Anderson Bridge and had an esoteric air about it, it gave one an intriguing impression. The large ramps that led from the boat bays to the water, the docks for coach-launches and the observation decks and flag masts all contributed to the effect that this was the center of a specialized activity — competitive rowing.

One entered the boathouse through two sets of oaken doors that folded open to permit the passage of long racing shells. To the front ran four bays of boats stacked floor-to-ceiling on racks – and beyond the racks four doors opened towards the river. On the far right was a repair shop and on the far left, two extraordinary rooms called rowing tanks. By pumping water through troughs past seated oarsmen, rowing conditions could be simulated in the indoor tanks. Oarsmen, consequently, could continue to train even when the river was frozen.

In the hallways just beyond the entrance doors there used to sit two machines called "ergometers." Knowing the rigor of the Harvard program I assume that these machines are still sitting there, and most likely, several others have been added.[2] The ergometer is a machine designed to measure an oarsman's performance on a minute-by-minute basis. An oar handle is attached to a ratchet gear that spins a flywheel. A loud "thunk" may be heard as the ratchet is engaged on the flywheel. After the pull-through the ratchet is released and the flywheel spins free. This produces a metallic clatter of disengaged gear teeth. Through winter nights one may hear "thunk, zing, thunk, zing, thunk, zing," as oarsmen work out on the machine. Accuracy of measurement is obtained by setting a counter on the flywheel to count revolutions.

There are stairs leading from both sides of the entrances to the second floor. Where there were boat bays before, here there is only one large exercise room. Rows of antiquated rowing machines of the sort one often sees in gymnasiums — oar handles in hydraulic shock absorbers — sit bolted to the floor.

What is immediately apparent to any visitor is this: trophies everywhere; on the walls, on the rafters, on the mantle, sitting on tables. Oars, cups, plaques, banners, medals, boat bows — all of them have been casually strewn about the boathouse and allowed to collect dust. It is as if to say, "We have won all that there is to win, but that is not what we are after. We are after the ineffable dream of the perfect oarsman." The perpetual clunk and zing of the torturous ergometer bears non-verbal testimony to this pursuit.

Rowing is one of the best settings I know for making fast friends. C. S. Lewis said that lovers stand face-to-face, and friends stand side-by-side; lovers are united by a common interest in each other; friends are united by a common interest in something else. The rowing environment provides an endless source of material for mutual sharing. The aesthetics of style, oars, boats and sensations; victories and defeats are the subjects of continuous debate. The oarsman in his capacity for true friendship is a lost breed in this mechanical world. For he is like the craftsman of older times who could both enjoy his craft and the fellowship of similarly skilled men. At the college we had nicknames for types of students. "Jocks", of course, were athletes; "wonks" were intense students; but "crew bore" was the title given to an oarsman — an appellation describing his excessive zeal for rowing, and in particular, to his daily shoptalk. We indifferently rowed through the East Coast electrical failure of 1967; the 1970 crew competed despite student strikes over Cambodia; and a recent oarsman said he'd walk off a cliff for his coach. Any serious oarsman had to face the fact that rowing would largely shape his college years. But the rewards of rowing were great too; not the least of which was sheer aesthetic pleasure.

I don't think one can underestimate the unique fervor oarsmen maintain for this sport. In 1898, a sophomore rowed at #4 on the varsity boat. A dozen years earlier he had received a letter from the captain of the crew entreating him to "go to Harvard and try for the crew." This early proselytizing brought Francis L. "Peter" Higginson, '00, to Harvard. In 1899 he was captain of the boat and again in 1900. In 1951 he organized "The Friends of Harvard Rowing" to solicit contributions from graduate oarsmen and other friends of the sport. In 1965 Mr. Higginson invited our freshman crew aboard his yacht for a cruise up the Thames River in New London, Connecticut. His fondness for crew had remained unabated.

It seemed, too, that this affection was maintained from one generation to the next. Nick Bancroft, class of 1963, rowed on the varsity boat as had his father, grandfather and great-grandfather – 'Foxey' Bancroft, '78. The father of a close crew friend had rowed on the crew thirty years before. One of my three roommates, John Crocker, proved to be a talented starboard man. His father had captained the 1941 lightweight varsity.

The Harvard-Yale race of August 3, 1852 (which Harvard won) was Harvard's first intercollegiate contest. It was also the first intercollegiate athletic event held in the United States. Our row with Yale in the spring of 1965 marked the 100th rowing of this race. In 113 years many improvements had been made in equipment and technique. However, the sport of rowing has changed very little in its fundamentals. Success in rowing is based on technique, conditioning and to a lesser extent on suitable equipment. Since the sliding seat came into general use in 1873, there have been few major improvements in equipment, though there have been many minor ones. The modern racing shell for eight men and a coxswain resembles its counterpart of a hundred years ago to a remarkable extent. It is a round-bottomed, keelless "shell," about 60 feet long, 25 inches wide at its beam, and has eight outriggers to hold the oars. The oar is 12-1/2 feet long.

To an outsider, rowing means a few colorful races in the late spring. For an oarsman, it is a way of life that begins in the fall, continues through the winter, and often lasts through the summer.

There are four parts to the stroke: the catch, the pull-through, the finish and the recovery. At the catch it is important to drop the oar in quickly by lifting your hands. During the pull-through, the back and legs are opening steadily, and the arms are keeping the oar buried at one even level. The finish requires that you reverse the direction of the stroke. Now, simultaneously, you must turn or "feather" the oar and push it away from your chest. This releases the oar from the water smoothly. If the stroke is performed grace-fully, it should look like a billiard ball hitting a cushion. You will see a level pull-through, a bounce at the finish and a level rollaway on the recovery. During the recovery it is important to keep the oar off the surface of the water. This means that the whole boat must be balanced and not rolling from side to side.

It is difficult for many people to believe that rowing is worth the effort and sacrifice. My doubts were dispelled one autumn evening of freshman year when I saw the varsity "Wonder Crew" of 1965 doing pieces between the Old Power House and the Boston University Bridge. Six members of that boat had gone to the Olympics, and they had soundly defeated all collegiate opposition the previous year. We freshmen were sitting at the Power House corner, waiting for our coach, when the Wonder Crew turned the bend. They were at three-fourths power and seemed to have plenty in reserve. I was most impressed by the razor sharp edge of conditioning and control that the crew had developed. Every catch hit the water at the same instant, with one terrific thrust all eight backs opened simultaneously, and then all eight oars released eight perfect puddles of energized, churning water — no more, no less than a perfect stroke. The boat leapt like a ballerina, and we sat in silent awe as over and over again the solemn oarsmen propelled their craft through the cool water. No other sounds were heard than the quick clap of the oars at the catch, a clatter at the finish, and then the hiss and boil of water along the shell's hull.

Glory is not the goal of rowing; stylistic perfection is. I have seen men cry in their seats because they were frustrated by poor style. I have also seen men vomit and faint from the effort exerted, or develop blood poisoning when their blistered hands became infected. It was pains like these that often produced a good crew.

For most of the freshman rowing season I rowed on the second boat as I had been beaten by John Crocker, my roommate, for a seat in the first boat. But before the first race against Rutgers and Brown, John strained his wrist, and I got an opportunity to start my rowing career as bowman for the first boat.

On the day of our race we had a good breakfast, rested, lunched on steak, rested again, and then headed down to the boathouse. Seven months of preparation were on the line. Our coach, Ted Washburn, nervously told us about the weather conditions, the strategy for the start and the final sprint. We were to row the body of the race at thirty-two strokes per minute. We knew very well that every stroke would count, that there would be no letdown or flagging in effort, and very likely we would face physical and mental pressures we had never before known. Then it was time to get the boat. Our coxswain conquered his fear, and with loud authority barked out orders: "Hands on the shell! Ready, lift! Shoulder high! Walk it out of the house!"

On the dock we saw Rutgers and Brown men looking very large. On race day the competition always looks imposing. You notice their size, their muscle development. "Their five man has forearms like hams," I said. A crowd of spectators had congregated on the dock along with the opposing teams.

"Over your head, starboard under!" our cox commanded. "Set her down gently, fix your foot bindings, get your oars." Oarlocks were tested and greased, oars checked, slides cleaned and oiled. Our coach gathered us together for a last word. "Men, I haven't eaten today because I haven't been able to. I'm eager for you to show your best. Keep it long and low. If you get an inch on them for every stroke you'll be twenty-four feet ahead by the finish. Relax on the recovery, but bust it when the oars are buried. Concentrate. If you're behind at the start, don't worry. Hold on to them and grind 'em down. Let's get our hands together and give a shout." We gave the closest thing to a prayer — a rising yell — and then boarded the shell.

"One foot on the dock, hands on the oars, ready, shove," the cox commanded, and we shoved the shell from the dock. "Sit, number two take a stroke." We were free from the dock. "All eight, ready to row, row!" With a surge of power that bent oars and tore large holes in the river surface we lunged away from the dock. The crowd cheered, and we were off, alone now in the boat to face our first challenge.

It was about four miles from the boathouse down to the starting line, and it took from forty minutes to an hour to warm up before a race. By the time we reached the start at the mouth of the Charles we were breathing hard and sweating freely. The race would be one and three-quarters miles that day. Usually, there will be stake boats at the start with boys to hold the shells on an equal line and aimed down the course. And so, the first job of the coxswain at this time is to maneuver his boat into position. Once the boats are even and aimed down the course you take off your sweats and suck on a lemon to activate salivary glands. Then the judges' launch comes over, and the judge asks: "Harvard, are you ready? If you are not ready, raise your hand, coxswain. Brown, are you ready? Rutgers, are you ready?"

When all boats are aimed on target, the judge says, "I will give you three commands: Are you ready? Ready, all. Row!"

And then he did and we did. Twenty-four oars strained off the starting line. From the banks it would have looked like three boats gradually getting up to speed, but in the boat itself things were happening too fast to think. "Short, short, short, long, long, long," I was thinking to myself. And the cox was screaming, "Long, long, long — lengthen it! Alright, ten high!" The cadence rose to a sizzling forty-two strokes per minute for ten strokes. And I heard, "Drop it for ten! And lengthen it!" Almost as if we were shifting into high gear in a car, the pace dropped to thirty-six strokes per minute for ten strokes. And then came the part of the race that I think is most exciting: the settle. All three coxswains were screaming at the top of their lungs when our command came across:

"Settle it! And lengthen!" This is the time when a boat comes down from the high short strokes of the start and begins to row at the cadence it will use for the body of the race. This is when the serious rowing begins, for most that a crew hopes to do will come from its ability to handle the boat at its racing stroke. When the command to settle came, I felt a sudden relaxation in the boat. The seats no longer screamed up the slides; instead they were almost floating in slow motion. It seemed as though we waited too long on the recovery before taking the next stroke. That is what "lengthening it" means. It means you take as long as you can between strokes to let the boat run on the water, but when you do take a stroke you pull it as hard as you can. It's like ice-skating where you take a great kick and then glide as long as possible until the next kick.

I had not looked out of our boat for the first minute of the race, but after the settle I saw Rutgers close to us with Brown several feet back.

Our Coxswain shouted, "You've got a seat on Rutgers and three on Brown, lengthen!"

Stroke by stroke we began to pull away from the opposition until we had a full boat length on Rutgers and about another half on Brown and we were increasing the lead.

Inexorably, the command came up to lengthen. "Number five, you're short at the catch. You're early, two."

With every command the boat hopped in the water, and it seemed we were getting more glide per stroke. At the finish line, Rutgers was four boat lengths behind us, or about two hundred forty feet. We had gained not one but ten inches on the opposition every time we put our oars in the water. Brown was another three lengths behind Rutgers.

I collapsed with fatigue at the finish, having rowed semiconscious for the last quarter mile. But soon a great peacefulness replaced the pain; and then I began to smile, splash water, and tell jokes with the other oarsmen. When we got back to the dock, I received the traditional tokens of victory: shirts from the Rutgers and Brown bowmen. And I learned that our time was only fourteen seconds behind the varsity time that day. But best of all would be the endless recounting of how well we had done — how rapid the start had been, how smooth the settle, how torturous the final quarter and how convincing the margin of victory. All over again we would earn the name "crew bores."

If you can imagine the thrill of one man winning one race, multiply that forty-five times and put it under one roof and you will have some idea of the excitement that stirred within the Harvard quarters that day. All five heavyweight crews went undefeated that day, and the next race day, and the next, and the next, and the next. Not a single collegiate crew finished ahead of the Harvard heavies that year.

Much of my identity at Harvard came from rowing, but it was a mistake. Underlying much laxity was the excuse that I rowed. If I did poorly on an exam, it was okay because I rowed. If a budding desire grew in my heart for drama, or music, or poetry I dismissed it on the grounds that rowing was my art as well as my sport. And I began to treat emotions with reference to crew. If I broke up with a girlfriend, I'd say to myself, "There will be a couple of lonely nights, but I'll get over it." The rigor of rowing, combined with Harvard's prestige in this sport, froze my heart to the mermaid cries about me.

Before the Charles thawed March of my sophomore year we were breaking and sawing the ice into large chunks and sending it down stream. And with cold winds numbing our fingers we began spring training on the water. It was a rebuilding year, since six members of the Wonder Crew had graduated. I was driving a 1959 black BMW motorcycle to and from practice and anticipating spring break when the hardest training would occur. At that time selections would be made for the various boats, and so each session on the water would be a grueling test of strength and endurance.

When spring vacation arrived, I was surprised to find myself a serious contender for the varsity boat. Although comparatively strong, I was three inches shorter and ten pounds lighter than the average contender. But once I whiffed a possibility of making first boat, visions of glory leapt to my head — travel in Europe, publicity, victory — and I promised to give it my all.

At the end of the vacation, Harry Parker, our coach gathered eight of us together at the end of the dock. "I want to talk to you eight. I'm convinced that you men are the strongest and most efficient on the squad. I've looked over your records for weight lifting, running, and your competition in boats during the year. Each of you shows an ability to move the boat you're rowing in. Together I think you can make a good crew." Harry's manner was thoughtful and understated. While we oarsmen kept sober faces, inside we exploded for joy. "And so I'm going to keep you together for our first race against Brown next week. We'll start rowing in the racing boat on Monday. Get plenty of rest this weekend and don't do anything foolish."

Too good to be true. I seemingly had awakened one morning to find myself at the very center of American rowing. To any other college crew I would represent the ineffable dream of the perfect oarsman. Of course, the challenge lay ahead to prove it, but for a moment my position as # four in the varsity seemed to transcend the gray realities of practice.

Our toughest contest that year proved to be our first race against Brown. Moments before the race, a young boy on a tricycle rode up to me and asked my name. Without a thought I had become Odysseus. "My name is Eric Sigward, Sacker of Cities," I replied. The crew burst into hearty laughter. "Alright, Sacker, baby," they chimed. My nickname was fixed.

I was relieved to have acceptance from the other guys because I was amazed to be rowing at this level, and shy about myself as a great Harvard oarsman. In particular, I thought our stroke, Clint Allen, was deriding me. Clint was the type of blonde god that made me nervous. A high school football star, he lived in Eliot house with the blue bloods. He drove a white convertible sports car and had a delicious girlfriend. Now he was stroke for the Harvard varsity crew. You can imagine him with a yellow sweater tied casually over his shoulders, white flannel trousers, and penny loafers but no socks, a girlfriend in the car. He had all the right moves. He was something out of F. Scott Fitzgerald. Clint played polo, flew planes, and made fortunes. He was Brooks Brothers when Brooks Brothers was Brooks Brothers. He was Ralph Lauren

Polo before there was a Ralph Lauren Polo. Thus, I was relieved when the whole crew laughed at my joke. A pecking order clicked on and I was in. Clint looked to Brian Clemow, an Olympian leftover from the previous year. With Brian's approval, I also got Clint's. I was now just an ordinary cool guy.

We beat Brown that day by only one length, Princeton the next week, and Penn the week after. Weekly my collection of shirts grew. Front page news in Boston read, "Heavy Crew Keeps Winning, Harvard Again." When we entered the Eastern Sprints the news read, "14 Crews Challenge Harvard." The Sprints were a repeat of my first freshman race. I opened by eyes after the start to find us a length up on the field with five other boats scrambling for second place. We were on the way to seeing Harvard's third straight undefeated season. We would see its fourth and fifth.

Before the June Yale race I received a call from my sister, Ellen. "Your father's dying," she said. "You'd better come home." "You're kidding," I replied. "What is it?" "He has leukemia." "I'll come home, but I have to get back here for the Yale race."

We would train for the Yale race, traditionally four miles long at Red Top, the crew's training headquarters in New London, Connecticut. The race, supposed to be a close one, lasted for only the first half mile where we went ahead to win by six lengths in an upstream record. As soon as the post-race partying was over, I mounted my BMW, and sped to New York where my father lay in the hospital.

I sauntered into his room with the headlines in my hand: "Harvard Outstrips Yale." "We're Number One," I said hopefully.

My father was jaundiced from the leukemia. His large, athletic frame looked cramped in the hospital bed. "I know," he said, "I saw you on television. It was the saddest day of my life; I wanted so much to be there to watch you."

He died eleven days later. Because he was proud of his American citizenship and his service in the Army, he requested a military burial. The night after his interment I drove through Manhattan, sobbing freely in the anonymity of city traffic.

Like dusty trophies, I promptly forgot the victories of sophomore year and entered junior year. A process of entropy and diffusion became evident with my father's death. I was more mature that year but also wildly extravagant. Debauching in the fall led to failure in organic chemistry, and winter I dropped from the pre-med program.

I could not see then that my life was fragmenting. "I row." The statement could justify infidelity to girlfriends, failure in chemistry, the abandoning of medicine. As spring practice commenced, it became crushingly apparent that I was fighting for my life as a first boat contender. I panicked under the pressure. It was well and good to be philosophical about the joys of rowing as a first boatman, but to be demoted to second boat brought philosophy to a personal level. All talk of teamwork and the common goal of Harvard eminence blurred before the thought that I was to be second boat. My small size and weight had caught up with me. A new year had brought up new, larger men from the freshman class, not to mention that my libertine ways had rotted some competitive moral fiber. By race time I found myself standing on the windy boathouse dock trying to convince Harry to let me back into the boat. I had been beaten by Cleve Livingston, a Californian, for a seat in the first boat, and would have to make the best of a second boat grind. That year we had a junior varsity filled with frustrated oarsmen. Without the necessary *esprit*, the boat sagged in the water.

"Incredible," however, was the comment of one coach who saw the 1967 Varsity. Like the Wonder Crew they soundly defeated all opposition and extended Harvard's winning streak to twenty-seven over a four-year period, a feat never before accomplished by any school. At the Eastern Sprints Harvard won by two lengths over Pennsylvania, considered the finest in decades. The entire collegiate rowing season could have been wrapped in one word — Harvard.

Summer of '67, despite a poor showing by our JV the previous season, Harry chose me to be an alternate for the upcoming international rowing. The varsity was training for the Pan American Games in Winnipeg, Canada, and the European Rowing Championships in Vichy, France. After winning the trials, the Harvard eight became the United States representative in that class for the Pan Am Games; and as such we marched into Winnipeg Stadium in red, white, and blue along with athletes from twenty-seven other countries. Our eight took a Gold Medal there and went on to Vichy where we came in second to the Germans. Andy Larkin, the six-man, maintains that the final in Vichy was the best race our generation ever rowed. The German eight from Vichy won the gold medal in Mexico the following summer.

With the experience of the summer behind me, I entered senior year. I had seen three consecutive years of victory by Harvard boats, and yet our sights were aimed for even bigger game in 1968: The Mexico Olympics. Winter two ergometers moved in, and all illusions about ourselves were dispelled. In cold numbers we saw our relative performances.

All along I had seen romantic notions about rowing replaced by technology. It was once held that technique, above all, was the key to successful rowing. I had heard old-timers talk about rowing as a gentlemanly pastime and a poetic experience of one's youth. When I entered Harvard, weight lifting had just begun to be a large part of our training program, but we were more concerned with the inexpressible beauties of the sport: a catch neither too fast nor too slow, a finish without splash.

Several years later, I would hear English coaches wax poetic in the old way when coaching a boat. "Lift the catch lightly as you would the hem of a dress," an English coach told us. "At the finish, caress your chest with the oar."

In England, rowing was still an excuse for bombast and rhetoric. At Harvard, however, a new era of rowing had begun. Harry Parker, youthful coach and innovator, would see the longest winning streak in the history of collegiate rowing. Harry abandoned the American Pocock shell for the shorter Swiss-made Staempfli. The 'shovel' or 'tulip' oar was first used successfully by

Harvard in 1963. Harry was the first American coach to try the German style of rigging a boat that places the 4 and 5 men on the same side. By Harry's initiative we adopted the German rowing style and interval training. Previously crews went for interminably long rows, accompanied by wordy coaching. Now rowing was scientifically geared to information about blood circulation and muscle characteristics. Maximum conditioning, it was found, occurred where the limits of stress were continually exceeded. A balance of hard strokes and recuperative strokes became the continuous format for our workouts. Rowing, in our era, developed from the hazy realms of poetry and gentlemanly aesthetic to a science of technique, conditioning, motivations and boat and oar construction. Senior year we would try for the Olympics, a feat never before accomplished by a Harvard eight; but my personal life was a shambles. Drinking beer and smoking pot with friends became magnetically enjoyable. I was smaller by comparison in my senior year as new oarsmen joined the ranks. A new girlfriend, the convicting ergometer, size problems, a growing sense that despite our new goals I had experienced much of what rowing had to offer — I quit. I could not face another morning workout, another defeat. It was time to retire my oar.

July 1968 Harvard won an Olympic berth, beating the University of Pennsylvania by four-hundredths of a second. Four inches! Time does not allow me to tell of Harvard's lackluster sixth place finish in the Mexico Olympics, but heat, altitude, and illnesses among all the athletes contributed to making competition unreliable and sloppy in that city. This was the first and last Harvard Eight to represent the United States in the Olympic Games.

What the experience of rowing has meant to me I can only begin to tell. There are glass-still mornings when you acutely feel the steady rhythm of the strokes, you hear the gentle rivulets falling from the oars. Harry pulls alongside in his launch and makes comments. The boat gains momentum. You pull more, and the boat speeds up, you pull harder and you feel the boat surging rhythmically. All you see is some guy's back straining in front of you.

"Power!" The coxswain screams, and you feel a magnificent burst of speed that takes you away from the water, the bleeding hands, and the slicing oars into the metaphorical realms of flight, and light, and love.

With the joy of the sport I had seen disillusionment, too. Neither a charismatic coach nor an inherently satisfying sport could heal the sting of defeat. I was cynical when I left Harvard because it took a horrendous leap of faith to believe that I had actually rowed for the good of the team and for the inherent goodness of the sport. When things got rough, I would not row in the second boat, I would not row for the good of the team. Therein lay the conflict: how to reconcile personal failure with lofty platitudes about the virtues of rowing. Only disillusionment and cynicism could be the honest result of that conflict. I had won a lot of races but was a bad loser.

That was my element,
war and battle. Farming I never cared for,
nor life at home, nor fathering fair children.
I reveled in long ships with oars; I loved
polished lances, arrows in the skirmish,
the shapes of doom that others shake to see.
　— Odyssey, *XIV (222-226)*

CHAPTER 4: SOCIALLY YOURS

And as where'ere the roses grow
Some rain or dew descends,
'Tis nature's law that wine should flow
To wet the lips of friends.
                    – Oliver Wendell Holmes

No one could miss the social implications of going to Harvard. To the thirty-some-odd schools in the Boston area Harvard was queen. The traffic jams into the Square each Saturday left no doubt that Harvard was a hub of life. C. Wright Mills had told me that the power elite started as a college club and later became the military-industrial-governmental complex. The Kennedy era and the economist John Kenneth Galbraith had convinced me that the university was parentally related to big business and the government. The hand that rocked baby ruled the world. College was that hand, and I was the baby. Therefore, I approached freshman year with the attitude that from among my classmates might very well come the senators or President of the future.

Linda and I had another encounter in freshman year. Since she was only 14 miles away, I pursued her once again at Wellesley. We fed each other's melancholy as we pondered the adolescent pressures of life. Her sad passions called to me like the great heroines of Wagner. She would one day write

> I think that it would be really good if sometime in the near future — only if you would want though. I don't want to bother you. I'd like so much really just to talk with you — I want you to under-

stand so many things that you don't now. I want to tell you who I am and why I act the way I do. I hope you will listen to me. I feel so helpless and bewildered. I'm trying to maintain certain human values — certain realistic hopes, and all seems to tumble down about me. I appeal to you, I beg you, please if ever you once liked me, to help me now — I want to explain myself — and then you may go away and leave forever and I shall know that there is nothing to save, now all is lost, save a tiny core of stillness in the heart like the eye of a violet. Once I thought that you felt as I did — that there was some kind of spiritual or intellectual bond between us. And perhaps there was. In memory of that former relationship, I beseech you, Eric, let me speak with you.

I wanted to be bothered by her. How at age eighteen she had acquired oceans of passion I don't know, but she had touched the flickering flames of joy and known personally both cavernous emptiness and blissful forgetfulness.

I had invited Linda to the Harvard-Yale Game freshman year, but she refused and sent her next-door neighbor, Shawn Murphy. If Linda was a sleeping Brunhilde, Shawn was a singing Rhine maiden. Like Keats's fairy child, 'Her hair was long, her foot was light.' Shawn had blonde hair and blue eyes. She was perfectly beautiful and a Catholic, a quirk I accepted disdainfully.

"But," she would say, "ironic, as it must seem to you, I believe my peculiar 'weakness' offers greater protection for you than your dark strength holds for me. It's so much easier to indulge in bitter rejection than to become involved in mankind actively. Strength is being unselfish."

She knew that I was intently searching for answers, and this was her offer of leading. While Linda was a perfect student, Shawn let studies ride for parties, luncheons, dances, and teas. A good little girl helping a melodramatic little boy, she played the fairy child and I the woeful knight.

Honor would not allow me to carry on two intense relationships, and I soon told Shawn that my heart, for what it was worth, belonged to Linda. Subsequently, Linda opted for freedom and I was left alone on the cold hillside.

Sophomore year included a romance with a Cliffie and an incomprehensible breakup. Quick-witted, Vivi was impatient with my ponderous glooms, and she left me for good one night at the door of her dormitory. But sophomore year was great for crew, for study, and for motorcycles. I purchased my 1959 BMW that year, the Rolls Royce of motorcycles, and drove it pleasurably for the next two-and-a-half years. Built for comfort, it would smoothly prowl the streets of Cambridge like a large black cat, or cruise from Boston to New York at 80 without a complaint. I studied Freudianism with moderate glee, for I appreciated the clarity and conviction of its insights, and did a case study of Freudian neurosis. And, as mentioned, I made the first boat that year.

After our race against Yale and the death of my father, Ian Gardiner wrote me a letter, "Eric, you are like a brother to me. I know it was tough holding on at Red Top when you knew your father was dying. Just want you to know that my folks and I really love you."

With the death of my father, the Gardiners became a kind of foster family. I rowed with Ian, and for several years went hunting with him and Mr. Gardiner at their farm in Gardiner, Maine. I learned of cigars, and hearty fun from the Gardiners. The spare New England wit flavored Mr. Gardiner's humor. "I did not send Mr. Roosevelt my *best* regards," he told me, "I sent him my *regards*."

The Gardiners lived for most of the year in a saltbox house in Topsfield, Massachusetts, but took outings to their farm in Gardiner. Mr. Gardiner belonged to several men's clubs in Boston, to the Friends of Harvard Rowing, and at that time he was Grand Marshall of the Porcellian Club. I was much taken by Mr. Gardiner's reputation as a Brahmin of Boston, as well as by his warmth and generosity. After practices I often gave Ian a lift to his rooms at Kirkland House, and one afternoon in the fall of junior year Ian asked me, "Siggy, what do you know about clubs at Harvard?"

"Not much," I admitted.

"Have you heard of the Porcellian Club?"

"Sure, I've heard it's the best. It was Teddy Roosevelt's Club".

"That's right, Siggy. How would you like to join the Porcellian?"

"What do I have to do?"

"Just wait, I'll ask the brothers to punch you this season, and we'll see what happens."

I went home to my rooms and asked Dick Grossman, my Bostonian roommate, what he thought of the Porcellian Club. "Eric! You've made it. The Porcellian Club is the most prestigious club in Boston. The Kennedys couldn't get in. They were *nouveau riche.*"

"Tell me more, Dick."

"I think Buffer Krebbs is an ass, and so is Nigel Kreef. They're a lot of rich asses. But there are some good guys, too, oarsmen: Tuffer Cutler, Terry Considine, and Ian."

"What do they do in the club?"

"You'll see." Dick passed into reverie for a moment. "My roommate, a Porc. That's the closest I'll ever get to the P.C. They eat and drink and make comments about the lower classes."

"Dick, do you think I'll get in?"

"Eric, when Ian Gardiner asks you to join the P.C., you'll get in. Mr. Gardiner is Mr. P.C."

I was punched by David Braga, which means I was dined at restaurants, clubs, and homes in the Boston area. Braga showed me how to buy a tuxedo and patent leather pumps for parties, where I was interrogated to see whether I could serve as one of forty current members.

I slept very poorly on election night in December, and by 8:00 AM the next morning was sure I had been rejected. Ian had been tightlipped for the previous few weeks, as had other members.

I did not have the prestigious family background, finances, or prep schooling that other members had. There were no real grounds for hope. At eight-thirty Ian came into my room looking wasted from a sleepless night.

"I guess I didn't make it," I said, not seeing any light in his face.

"Come here, Siggy. This is for you." He handed me a parchment envelope with a green boar's head on the flap. "I have the honor of informing you," he said, "that you have been elected to the Porcellian Club. However, it is not customary for me to congratulate you at this time." He shook my hand, grinned broadly, handed me a cigar, and walked out. In the envelope I found my formal invitation to join the club along with a list of new members.

Just what was the Porcellian Club? It was, as close as I can compare, like a king's court of older times. Venerable men, scholars, athletes came to the club to talk, read, eat, or play. It was the scene of high conversation, strong drink, tobacco, courtesy, merriment, and bawd. We ate daily lunches in the club, as well as monthly dinners and traditional feasts. I learned there the proper place of pomp and ceremony — that there are times when ritual awakes simple emotions of happiness, such times when selfish joys and griefs are submerged under tradition. I admit that in this sense the prosaic molds into which we place our lives can have dignity and meaning. The so-called American dream which I had chased was valid insofar as it produced purpose and beauty which would not have existed had I not submitted myself to higher callings.

The club, which was founded in 1791, overlooked Massachusetts Avenue and the Yard. The clubhouse contained a library, several reading rooms, a kitchen, dining room, and a game room. The mahogany walls were lined with endless pig and boar figurines — some in jade, silver and ivory. Over the library table hung Teddy Roosevelt's spurs.

On initiation night, we new members were dressed in jockey

suits, complete with silk vests and caps embroidered with silver boars. An older member led me into the club, but before I got through the front door I saw Dean Skiddy Von Stade pass before me.

"I didn't know he was a member," I thought.

As I myself entered the front room I heard him say, "Brother Canham, what's that one's name?"

"Initiate Sigward, Brother Von Stade."

"Be especially hard on him, he tried to push me into a puddle as I was entering the club."

"Usual thing, Brother Von Stade."

I was blindfolded, led upstairs, and seated in an overstuffed chair. I could hear raucous, bellowing, festive voices about me; and immediately I was barraged with unanswerable questions and impossible demands. Before and after dinner I was tutored in club customs. For instance, under no circumstance was a female permitted to enter the club above the downstairs foyer.

I went home drunk that night and fell asleep on the floor. In the next year I learned the club customs regarding food, drink, dress, and use of the clubhouse. I met wealthy men, partied at old mansions, and listened to conversations about magnates, governors, and men in the highest places.

Aside from being friends, some of these men were simply platonic images to me, pure entities of their own type. It was impossible, for instance, for me to imagine Volney Foster, our portly undergraduate president, in any other context than Harvard and the Porcellian Club. Full-fleshed, warm, kind, surrounded by men of power and intelligence, he seemed almost a voluptuary Samuel Johnson. He was a good British historian and hilarious as bosomy women in Hasty Pudding Society musicals. Talent rolled from him like oriental carpets. He belonged in mahogany clubrooms with brass bars and long mirrors and as a graduate he migrated to Wall Street with young clubmen like himself.

Junior year I met a girl with whom marriage seemed feasible.

Peta was four feet eleven inches tall, a mere tadpole of a girl. I wooed her with charm, intellect, and physical power. In return she gave me loyalty, concern, and trust. She looked to me for protection and wise counsel.

Life was enjoyable with Peta, my tadpole. We lazily paddled through the pond of Harvard parties and social events. I patiently told her grand stories about Reality, the Importance of Reason, the Meaning of Suffering. I would be more cautious now. And I smiled ruefully at her exuberance, her inaccuracies, and misconceptions. I chortled at her logic.

One day I told her I would go to seek my fortune alone. She responded with crazy spinning and wild acrobatics. She gathered my words in a book and gave them back to me, wrote a story for me, and followed me to England. "You're getting there," I offered her, "but I'm going off without you." She swam off, laid her head down somewhere, and cried because her heart was breaking.

Ironically, I had achieved urbanity. My experiences on the crew, in the club, and in classes gave me the polish and savvy that the world calls success. In the summer of junior year, following Vichy, I toured Vienna with the Gardiners. The crew was standing in the Boston airport waiting to disembark for France when Mr. Gardiner approached me.

"Eric, how would you like to go boar hunting with us in Vienna?" I swallowed in disbelief. "Yes, of course I would like to go."

And so after the races in Vichy, Ian, his parents and I did an evening in Paris and a week in Vienna. There were no boar in the Vienna area, however, and so instead of hunting we toured the city.

Senior year 1967: senioritis. Do as little as you can to get by. Do a thesis. Beat the draft. Row. Plan for next year. Carl Thorne-Thompson bought my Harley; then was drafted and shot in Vietnam. While maintaining radio contact during a firefight, he exposed himself and was killed. Grass was coming in, and so was Batman. Psychedelic posters, ultra-violet lights and a stroboscope decorated our room.

I took a course called Social Relations 120, interpersonal relations. Social Relations 120 met in an oval room that had an amphitheater for spectators placed behind a one-way mirror. For an hour on each of three mornings our class met to discuss an amorphous body of sociological literature and to live for the spectators behind the glass wall. It was projected that we would develop scientific theories on the meaning of personality and social relationships. I am not enough of a philosopher to understand why we made so little progress toward these goals. Our opinions, sensations and feelings did not lead us to objective truth despite our attempts to create and arrange data. At best we could come to subjective and self-centered statements.

"Who is the leader in the class?" One Harvard junior might ask.

"Dan is, he's leading us to meaningful relationships", a student answered.

A week later he would say, "I had hoped he would be a leader, but he's not, he's too defensive; and I'm disappointed with him."

We treated the bubbles of our consciousness as if they were reality itself and never approached the question of truth that existed beyond our personalities.

We failed to arrive at any objective statements concerning life. However, I met a beautiful young lady in that class; but for some disturbing reason our love story did not materialize as we experienced stubborn, annoying differences.

Judy stood almost six feet tall, had a shock of hair like a mane and carried herself with dignity. Intellectually devastating, she seemingly defended the stronghold of her personality against all comers. In addition to definite political views, she maintained a stiff and often biting women's lib perspective on life. Since women may be as skillful as men in many areas of thought and work, she held, they should be treated as moral, sexual, and intellectual equals with men. Practically speaking, Judy believed that men held an unfair advantage over women vocationally and sexually.

For instance, jobs are more available and more lucrative for men than for women. Likewise, since men enjoy sex without suffering the consequences of pregnancy, why shouldn't women have the same freedom? She proved to be prescient considering the wide acceptance of these beliefs today.

"On a one-to-ten pain scale," Judy once explained, "childbirth is ten. A man hardly ever experiences that kind of pain. Why should a man have freedom from pregnancy and not a woman?"

Contraception and abortion seemed the rights of women, much as sex without pregnancy was a fact for men. To Judy's credit she carried her beliefs to Beirut after graduation, where she studied Arabic and French and traveled. At the U.N. she would determine policy for the Population Council on women's roles, reproductive health, and defining the adolescent period.

Judy disliked the Porcellian Club, naturally, because it was for men only. However, I felt our differences lay deeper than the club or the facts of sexual discrimination. Although her thinking was correct insofar as women being intellectually and morally men's equals — taking classes with Cliffies amply proved that — I instinctively distrusted several of her practical conclusions. Her vision of sexual and vocational equality destroyed for me the traditional images of father and mother, protector and protected, knight and lady. There lay something deeper in the makeup of men and women, some difference in the very maleness and femaleness of beings that demanded respect.

I did not doubt that Judy was my equal or better in many areas. However, I could not concede equality at the deeper levels of our relationship. I resented her making important decisions or initiating plans. There were real differences, I saw, in the roles we played as man and woman. I had courted her, not vice versa. There was no admitting that she had been the aggressor. I had worked nights to pay bills and date her. I opened doors, protected her on streets, paid for dinners and despite my efforts to appear modern, I was inwardly crushed to find she disliked cooking, housework and the thought of childbearing.

To be sure, I was a child playing the part of a true lover. I wanted comfort; she wanted the promise of growth and stability. I wanted my ego satisfied; she wanted love. She was politically sophisticated; the extent of my sophistication ended with respect for the President. She had friends of intellectual and social standing in America and Europe; I was a kid from New York. And so we fought — bold, brutal, masculine fights.

In Judy's fierce opposition she gave dignity to our friendship. With her, at least, there was no illusion of compatibility. We simply and continuously opposed one another. Before I went up to Cambridge University, we spent about a week together in Rome, and then parted.

An esoteric pleasure came to Harvard in my senior year. Instead of bright lights, tinkling glasses and animated conversation, the lights were dimmed, and in the tense silence a precious pipeful of marijuana passed from hand to hand. With marijuana time seemed suspended, sights and sounds rolled through one's mind like waves in caverns. One felt euphoric giddiness and often hallucinated having heightened artistic or musical ability. I will not go beyond this description, for to some extent, those who know what marijuana does, know. Those who don't, don't. Those who know can never fully explain the sensation to those who don't.

Though I greatly ignored the political changes taking place around me, I could not be totally unaffected by them. Shortly before graduation, Martin Luther King, Jr. and Robert Kennedy were assassinated. At graduation we wore black armbands over our academic robes to protest the war in Vietnam and to mourn for King and Kennedy. Mrs. King took the place of her husband as our Class Day speaker; and in an emotion-charged speech, criticized President Johnson, churches, and the general adult population for their indifference to the violence in our lives.

"The young understand this society better than their elders think" she said, "and better perhaps even than their elders themselves."

Our final day of Harvard was marked by sadness — both

over the deaths of two leaders and over the prospect of fighting a war that ninety per cent of the seniors said they opposed. We had entered Harvard with an assassination, and were now exiting with two more.

The idealistic hopefulness that characterized my entrance into Harvard had taken an about-face. I was leaving Harvard to meet perhaps, a violent death. The war challenged the whole American society; and the University with its business and government connections was a part of the whole rotten mess. Napalm had been invented in Harvard laboratories. The old Harvard of rock-solid tradition and excellence was directly related to the deaths of thousands in Vietnam. And the weight of responsibility for honesty and change rested on our youthful shoulders. Youth itself seemed the answer; for apparently only students were free of the racism and materialism that corrupted the rest of the society. In this belief was foreshadowed the youth generation of flower children, free love and esoteric religions.

At graduation I received Harvard's equivalent of the Rhodes scholarship, the Lieutenant Charles Henry Fiske, III, Fellowship for two years of study at Trinity College, Cambridge — the richest social and intellectual climate in the world. Despite the war and the tragedies surrounding it, I was still insulated from personal trauma by Harvard's wealth and by yet another dream of adventure. I sold my motorcycle and picked up the remains of my Harvard life — books, suits, pipes, pot, oars and letters. I had avoided the draft because of my dislocated shoulder, and I received honors in General Studies.

The self-importance of a Harvard education was upon me. I was, by tradition, called to lead major innovations in society. It was the manifest destiny of a Harvard man.

"Harvard, Harvard, Harvard, Harvard, Harvard," we sang. It seemed all. But where was it? What was it? Where did its power lie? In the ceaseless shuffling of ideas? In the social relations class with no answer but Judy?

III) CAMBRIDGE UNIVERSITY

CHAPTER 5: FIRST IMPRESSIONS

Unmoved I could not always lightly pass
Through the same gateways, sleep where they had slept,
Wake where they had waked, range that enclosure old,
That garden of great intellects undisturbed.
— Wordsworth, *The Preludes*

The first six weeks of the summer of '68 I became a vocational counselor for a social work agency. Each morning I solicited jobs from local businesses for unemployed young men and women. I learned that what separated me from the habitually poor was not so much difference in ability as difference in restraints. I had grown up, not with greater talents, but with certain social advantages. Among these I would list alarm clocks, telephones, and discipline in routine. Insurmountable problems at home prevented our clients from maintaining their jobs — problems like heroin addiction, illegitimacy and lack of repression of violent impulses.

At the vocational office I met Gil Eisenberg, an aspiring Ph.D. in psychology with an empathetic heart towards the youths he daily faced. My correspondence with him over the Cambridge years helped me to clarify the direction of my thinking.

August I flew to Rome to meet Judy, having studied Italian for a month with Berlitz. As I sat in the airport waiting room with my mother on the night I left, I contemplated the leap I was about to make into Europe and Cambridge. I had set my sights on Europe and a Grand Tour. But before I could board the plane, a telegram reached me.

"The draft has rescinded the exemption," I said to my mother.

I felt relief when I realized it was a last-moment note from Gil wishing me a *bon voyage*

I boarded the plane that shortly took off into the night. In the previous summer I had descended upon the red-tiled roofs of southern France. What, I wondered, would the landscape of Italy look like?

In the bright morning we began our drop into Rome: small hills, brown dust, poplar trees like fingers and not as green as France. After customs, I started my Berlitz Italian.

"*Dov'e il banque?*" I asked the closest porter.

"*Va a la derecha, e poi a la sinistra.*"

The rhythms of the language flowed smoothly. My mother's Sicilian blood made me half-brother to these delicate, dark people. It was a hot Roman day but dry and comfortable. I took a bus from the airport to the city and then another bus to the Piazza di Spagna where I would meet Judy. '*Dov'e*' the Italian phrase for 'where is' became the primary survival phrase in Italy. Where is the Piazza? Where is the bus? Enough '*dov'es*' could get you anywhere.

"*Dov'e la signorina Americana,*" I asked the hotel manager, "Judy Bruce?"

"Seventeen," he replied in Italian.

At Judy's door I mimicked, "*Signorina, che il managero.*"

"*Si, Si, momento,*" I heard Judy chime from the room. She opened the door with the look of a woman much troubled by hotel service. "Eric! What a surprise! Oh, I've missed you so!" And she hugged me. After several minutes of conversation, Judy asked what I wanted to do.

"I'd like to see the Coliseum. But what would you like to do, Judy?"

"I've always dreamt of taking a ship from a Mediterranean port to Beirut. Would you like to join me and then fly back to Cambridge from Lebanon? The islands of Sicily, Crete, and Cyprus lie between Italy and Beirut."

Money forbade it. "Oodle, doodle, I'd like to relax and then take a walk."

"Yes, darling, of course. It's good to see you. I love you very much."

Judy lay back on the bed and read *Time* magazine, occasionally cursing Johnson and the war. I began to unpack and read the *Michelin Guide to Italy*. After a nap of several hours we located a restaurant in our guidebook.

Dressed at eight, we walked out into a cool Italian evening. Our hotel lay a block behind the *Piazza di Spagna*. At the base of the Spanish Steps sat an ancient fountain, shaped like a rowboat. Centuries of pouring water had colored the marble blue and green.

Judy had on a pink evening dress and white shawl. Her statuesque figure and serene manner made me proud. Already several of the single Italian males were eyeing us and making comments. How strange to think that I might have been on the street eyeing Judy instead of accompanying her.

At dinner Judy recounted her tour through Europe thus far: the American Embassy in London, a stay on the Left Bank in Paris, Antwerp, Grasse, St. Tropez, Valencia, Barcelona, Pamplona, and now Rome. She had seen shops, markets and galleries. In the future lay Israel and study in Lebanon.

I envied her flashing intellect, her comfort among the jet set, and her courage to plan and act independently. At Radcliffe she had been the center and queen bee of a coterie of friends — men and women of brilliance and social standing. I felt that I belonged more with the street rabble than with her. How could I ever overcome the sense of who I really was — a jock, a crew bore, a plodding student?

"You know what I'd like to do, Judy? I'd like to get a motorcycle and some sleeping bags and tour Italy by bike."

Judy was stung. "I really couldn't sleep out in a sleeping bag," she replied. "I hate roughing it — and what would I do with sixty pounds of belongings? You could camp out and I would take a cheap room."

"Judy, I could buy a small Fiat tomorrow and we could tour in it."

"Where would you want to go?"

"I'd like to see Naples, then head north to Florence and Venice."

"But I have to be in Israel by the end of the month. Let's see if you can get the car first."

The next morning Judy and I breakfasted on cappuccino and croissants, and while Judy rested I strolled to the Coliseum. It was huge, but unexpectedly old. Too much time separated me from its gladiatorial heyday: the Holy Roman Empire, the Dark Ages, the Renaissance, Modern Europe, and America. The old rocks could be little more than suggestions of former grandeur. I walked from the Coliseum to the Forum to see where Caesar had been stabbed on the Senate steps. Between the Coliseum and the Forum lay the ruins of Augustus Caesar's palace and the hill on which he assassinated rivals. From the top of that hill I looked across to the Circus Maximus, the site of chariot races. Only a large, dim shadow of an oval was visible beneath the dry grass, and occasional stones reminded one of the previous stadium.

Julius, Augustus, Caligula, Claudius, and Nero were growing fresher in my mind. Their visions of world-law and government, cities served by roads and aqueducts, aroused my own sense of purpose and destiny. Why had they failed? How would I find my fate?

I returned to the room to find Judy alert, cheerful, and writing letters. For lunch we bought some bread, cheese, tomatoes and salami and made a picnic. After lunch we learned that it would be prohibitively expensive to get a Fiat out of the country, and so Judy and I resolved to spend a week in Rome together and then go our separate ways to Israel and England.

On mornings Judy and I would walk through the streets of Rome enjoying the sights. Italians, it seems, have a flair for color, warmth, beauty and life. Everywhere one turns in Rome there is evidence of lively art. The fountains, for instance, depict turtles, fish, girls, men and seahorses. We rested in the afternoons, and ate in the evenings, often taking ice cream in the Piazza Navona next to the Bernini fountains.

Judy and I parted as she flew to Jerusalem and I rode to Naples with two Horace Manners I met in Rome. From Naples we drove to Sorrento and caught a boat to Capri. Vaguely relieved to be free from Judy's urbane ways I was now a vagabond in Europe. As the ferry from Sorrento churned towards Capri I noticed something strange. The blue water was splashing against the white prow of the boat, but it wasn't leaving any stain. How strange, I thought, blue water should stain a white boat. And then it hit me. This was the bluest water I had ever seen, so blue that you would think someone had dropped Tintex in it. "Oh, my gosh, this is the wine-dark sea of Odysseus."

From the town of Capri we hiked overland to the Blue Grotto and slept on a cliff overlooking the Mediterranean. In the morning we changed into swimsuits and climbed down steps in the cliff to where the surging sea rose and fell at the mouth of the cave. "If there's no grotto in there, we'll be smashed to bits against that hole," I said. We dove into the sea anyway, and swam towards the opening in the cliff. We swam into air, it seemed; and I had a giddy, silly feeling. For as we entered the cave all light came streaming from the ocean floor instead of from the sky. The cave was illuminated by light refracted through the water below, giving one the suddenly awe-inspiring feeling that ocean depths were full of life and light.

Back in Naples I met two enjoyable French girls. Irene's father published Beckett in Paris, and so she tended to be ethereal and existential. Veronique, on the other hand, was neat and agreeably piquant. At the Naples youth hostel I bought a motorcycle from a disenchanted American and began my drive to London.

London
September 15, 1968

Dear Gil,

Sorry to have delayed correspondence so long, but I think you deserve a letter rather than the usual scribbled postcard.

Perhaps the best thing you or anyone has told me is to trust my instincts. Thanks to you, my life has resisted the unnatural repressions and is now at least partially libidinal.

In other words, I spent nine square days with Judy and have made tracks ever since Rome in the cool world. Naturally Judy and I exploded, and I still harbor many destructive emotions toward her. Nevertheless, Rome was splendid and I hitched from there to Sorrento, boated to Capri, and slept atop the Blue Grotto, where I went swimming in the morning.

Rained constantly in sun-baked Naples and Pompeii, but there I bought a motorcycle (350-cc BSA) from a starving Columbia student and have been riding ever since with your shoulder bag on the front.

Have seen Florence and Venice, and my Italian has stood the test, even when explaining what's broken with the motorcycle. Love Italy tremendously and hope to revisit the country, churches and museums soon.

From Venice to Geneva, very cold and rainy on the St. Bernard Pass, countryside of Switzerland was like living in your electric-train set. Everything is perfectly placed to create an enchanting reality.

Geneva was a drag and took off for Lausanne where I ate lunch with a Scot who offered use of his tent for a bike ride to Grenoble.

Grenoble was a complete drag, architecturally and geographically in comparison to Italy.

Sped to Paris in a mercurial eleven hours where I took lodging in the house of a Parisian girl I met in Naples. Paris is quite delightful when you have a pretty escort and a home to stay in. Quickly engaged in Cafe society of the Latin Quarter and in student demonstrations. Though there are many protests and many radicals, France seems to take them as matter-of-fact and status quo.

Stung myself from Paris to London in thirteen hours (oh, my back!). In London took residence at very reasonable, though stuffy and moribund, Oxford-Cambridge Club. The porter thought I worked here yesterday for my lack of dark suit and tie. You know my style. It adds to the excitement to be thought of as the barbaric American. I do miss meeting people, though. There were so many at the hostels when I traveled dirty, with your bag on my shoulder. Now there's rain and my room and a copy of *Edward Gibbon and His World*. But I enjoy the solitude and will see much theatre. Write Trinity College. Waiting.

Eric

Peta had followed me to London from Boston, and one evening I received a call from her at the Oxford-Cambridge Club. She disguised her voice, making believe she was an English nurse who had met my mother in New York. I was surprised to find Peta when I called at her hotel room. We spent several days in London, buying clothes and sightseeing, and then I went up to Cambridge.

When I arrived at Trinity College, a porter in a black suit and bowler hat showed me to my rooms in the College.

"Mr. Hoffman comes back to visit us once in a while," the porter said while unlocking the door. "He was one of the best Fiskes we've had, won his oar on the University boat."

The doors to my suite opened onto a small hall. Behind the hall lay my bedroom, and to the left of the bedroom and hall I had a study.

"In this cupboard, sir, you'll find the Fiske silver and plates.

The porter pointed to a small cupboard to the right of the door. "Looks like Mr. Blume left his gown. You'll wear that to meals, meetings with your tutor, and to exams."

I looked at the short academic robe which was spotted with food and followed the porter into the study.

"They've just put central heating in this past year, so your rooms should be warm enough. If they're not, there's a gas fire in the fireplace. Twist the knob to the left to ignite, and to the right to adjust the flame. Some men like to toast bread on their fires; just put the pieces on the grid. I see they've brought your trunk up. In the stairway hall there's a kitchen for you, Mr. Troughton and Mr. Dawes, your neighbors. Mrs. Moore will clean your rooms every morning at nine. If you want your shoes shined or clothes cleaned, leave them at your door and Mr. Clarke will pick them up. There's a buttery next to the Hall for wines and liquors, a grocery store over the Old Kitchen, and the cooks will prepare meals for your rooms if you tell them in advance. I think that's all, Mr. Sigward, let us know at the Porters' Lodge if we can help you."

As he left, I stared at the scene of new adventures. On the right wall hung a large print of Harvard *circa* 1776 with familiar puritan buildings of red brick and white trim. Over the fireplace in front of me hung an oaken triptych shrine — a mantelpiece with a central panel and two flanking panels half its size that folded over it. The names and dates of previous Fiske Scholars had been carved on the wall and doors of the triptych. My desk sat on the left in front of two windows that faced Gaius and the gothic towers of Kings College.

Letters from my Harvard roommates and Judy had arrived at Trinity ahead of me. Dick was in Colorado doing high altitude training with the crew for Mexico and planning for law school. It looked like he would always remain in the Boston-Harvard mold. John was in the Army learning to fight.

> Letter from John Crocker
> October 20, 1968
> Fort Polk, Louisiana

Dear Eric,
Glad to hear you are seeing Peta again. I think

much of the joy and sadness in the room this spring was due to her alternate presence and absence. She was so thoughtful and considerate of all of us — hardly the pedestal complex of the other. I don't know how close you can ever really get to Judy. I fear that I project a lot of my own failings onto her, but her stylized model's life just didn't leave any room in it for you.

But, I suppose you know better than I how the relationship failed, and all I can say is that it seemed inevitable. You and Judy made the model couple in the fraternity society of suburban America; but in the adventure we all hope to live, Peta has the right touch.

As for the service — I screamed out loud in formation when I read "unfit for military service" in your letter and nobody was at all upset.

The M-16 rifle is an amazing weapon, incredibly accurate and fast. Likewise, the M-60 machine-gun. Tell me if you expect to be back in the States at all, and when, and keep up the correspondence. I too miss the nonsense and general disrespect of our life in Cambridge. But even thinking too hard about it will screw my mind when training starts each day.

John

Tommy, our writer roommate, had spent his summer playing the horses in New York. Then he moved to California to study and teach writing at Stanford.

Letter from Tom Ireland
October, 1968
Palo Alto, California

Dear Eric,

This can wait no longer. I tried once before, but my spirits are so volatile that anything I wrote one day would be false the next. It's no fun being stable, anyway.

I'm trying to imagine what you are now, 'a man of business, a man of expense, from shop to shop, to tutor or to tailor, as befalls, from street to street with loose and careless mind.' What really goes on beneath 'Trinity's loquacious clock'? With whom does Conan score tonight? When will he lay down his sword for saner pursuits?

If it could only last. . . I play my games well here, so well; in fact, that I'm winning back part of myself that has slept for too many winters. And when I live the way I know I should, I always think to myself, 'Eric would be proud of me.' California provides undreamed of opportunities for suffering, if you only know how to counteract its comfortable aspects.

Made it x-country on the BMW in six days, dear bicycle, I shall not call you bike, you proved yourself a veteran. I even got to ride with the 'Northern Rebels' along the Pacific the other day.

Pray for me, Eric.

What will become of us all? You and I are sure to lose our minds. This is all just midnight joy, and there's a long night ahead, full of megamorphic dreams.

More soon, Circe calls
Tom

Judy wrote a sweet letter from her new home in Beirut.

Letter from Judy Bruce
September 18, 1968
Beirut, Lebanon

Dear Eric,

I'm so happy. I have found a fantastically beautiful apartment overlooking the sea, surrounded on three sides by a terrace on the highest point on the coast, the top floor for $50 a month. All my friends are nonplused at my luck. I am now in the business of furnishing it, which can be done cheaply — labor is nothing so I will have everything handmade.

I think of you often. I hope you think of me. I loved Rome with you.

Love,
Judy

I didn't write Judy because I considered our relationship terminated in Rome. I had set my heart to leave her and wanted a clean break. However several months of guilt followed my fickleness.

Henry VIII founded Trinity College in 1546 when he amalgamated two earlier colleges, the older one dating from 1317. Whereas Harvard had seemed old before, now it seemed youthful and provincial by comparison. In the days before term started, I wandered through the town of Cambridge with its medieval streets and gentle Cam River; and I surveyed the Cambridge Colleges with their barbered lawns and patterned gardens. Like Harvard, the University is divided into separate colleges where most of one's life, save classes, takes place. Classes themselves meet at one's faculty site. The economics site, for instance, lies on the other side of the Cam River about half a mile south of Trinity. What is most unlike Harvard, however, is the surrounding countryside. Only several hundred yards behind New Court of Trinity sprawl open fields and fens. Whereas Harvard is surrounded by warm city lights and the civilization of New England, Cambridge is an isolated fortress that rises out of farmland and marsh.

My first impressions of Trinity included gathering information of previous residents, the most celebrated being Sir Isaac Newton. Others included the poet Byron and Sir Francis Bacon. And I learned that one of my classmates would be Prince Charles, heir to the throne of England, who would live only several hundred feet from my rooms.

My dream included fame, but my American presumptuousness palled before the history of Cambridge. The greatest intellects had played their roles on the Cambridge stage. In recent times, men like Keynes in economics, Darwin in physiology, the Huxleys in biology and literature, had greatly influenced modern thought. In older days there had been Erasmus in divinity, Malory in literature, and many others who changed the world from their scholars' stalls. It is no wonder that people believe in ghosts. These men, their thoughts and lives, lived as a presence in the lecture halls and libraries.

By the first week of October I was fairly well acquainted with Trinity College and Cambridge, and was awaiting the arrival of my friend from Harvard, John McKinnon, who had won a parallel scholarship to the Fiske for Emmanuel College. He would lodge in John Harvard's Elizabethan rooms. In the meantime I had learned to punt, or pole, a flat-bottomed boat on the Cam.

Peta wrote from London to say she was taking sociology at the University of London and had been accepted by Boston University to do a Ph.D. in English. She was spending time with an African financier named Joel, who claimed to have been a Don at Balliol, Oxford, was about 50, divorced, and had a hilarious upper crust humor. He invited me to a party once, saying, 'They'll have a bash at the Club this year. We'll get plastered, dance, and fight in the streets. It's quite formal, you can wear your dress uniform and medals if you like." Peta reported that Joel had asked permission to see her.

"I told him," Peta said, "if you appeared in the blackness of his room while he was sleeping with a three-foot machete knife in your teeth, a cleaver in your right hand and a whip in the left then no, I wasn't allowed. I warned him that *double* prayers would hardly help, so we agreed to keep a table between us."

October 6, 1968 was a clear, sunny, Cambridge day. I bought a bottle of wine from the Trinity Buttery that morning and walked over to John's rooms at Emmanuel to welcome him to Cambridge. I found him unpacking luggage in his oak-paneled rooms.

John stands about six feet five inches tall, and would have

been a great oarsman if he had rowed beyond freshman year. As it was, he turned from athletics to academics. He had been a gifted mathematician in high school, Phi-Beta-Kappa'ed English at Harvard, studied economics at Cambridge, and is presently an M.D. psychotherapist. He typified the kind of thoroughly skilled individual that Harvard attracts.

After wine and reminiscing, we walked out of Emmanuel and took a right down St. Andrew's Street towards the river and a pub lunch.

"How would you like to go punting, John?" I asked.

"What's punting?"

"You pole a flat-bottomed boat down the river. It's lovely."

"Sure, why not?"

We had gone a block when two girls walked past. I turned to John "Why don't we ask them to come with us?" John smiled. We spun around and ran towards the girls. "Do you want to come punting with us?" I asked. They turned to one another, smiled; and in a strange, lilting, guttural language, held a caucus.

"What's punting?" the darker one asked with a lovely accent.

"You do it with a pole on a boat," I explained, mimicking the procedure.

Again there was a momentary caucus in that strange language, and they turned to us, smiled, and said yes.

We introduced ourselves and they themselves. The taller, darker girl was Johanna; the slightly shorter blonde was Mudi. They were language students from Denmark, learning English in Cambridge. We picked up a punt at Magdalene Bridge, and poled south on the river past St. John's, Trinity, Clare, and King's Colleges. We propelled the gently moving craft under bridges and through overhanging weeping willows. John moved into the bow seat next to Johanna, and together they smiled up at me as I poled from the stern. Beneath me sat a cool looking young girl. John offered Johanna a cigarette, which she accepted. He took a paddle from the bottom of the boat and began to row with it. I looked at Mudi. She was quite attractive with long blonde hair, blue eyes, and an excellent figure. John looked at Johanna with approval. She had brown hair, brown eyes, and a pleasant Scandinavian form. They were both very beautiful, in fact. I looked to John. Johanna looked to Mudi. We all began to smile and laugh approvingly. We cruised back to the dock taking inept turns at moving the barge. After lunch we agreed to meet again for dinner. They would cook for us at Trinity in two days.

John and I walked back to my rooms in glory. It was too good to be true. We had been friends at Harvard — rowing, sharing, and carousing. Now here we were free in Europe, Cambridge students, richly endowed by our Harvard scholarships, and we had just met two of the most beautiful girls.

Letter to Gil Eisenberg
October 8, 1968

Dear Gil,

Cambridge life has picked up incredibly and beautifully. I get drunk more than I ever have in my life, with lusty pleasure. In addition, I have an absolutely exquisite Danish girlfriend who will be cooking dinner for me and a good friend tomorrow. My Gosh! She's wonderful.

I think I shall have to marry one of these incredibly feminine Scandinavians. I am 'being' more than ever in my life. I have more freedom than I have ever known and I love it.

You sound a bit lonely. I hope this cures itself soon, as I am sure it will because you are such a valuable person in all senses of the word. I bought the Dvorak and listen to it all day. It's wonderful. Thanks for the recommendation and as always thanks for support of my erratic life-style.

Wish you were here,
Eric

"A loaf of bread, a jug of wine, a book of verse, and thou," I was faithfully following Omar Khayam's recipe for contentment.

Eigenhändige Namensunterschrift des Inhabers:

**My father, Hans Siegwardt, 23, poses for
driver's license photo in Hamburg, Germany (1928).**

Angela Cosumano, my mother, is in the center, her parents are on the right, and her little sister Gerry is on the bottom, Brooklyn (c. 1926).

Hans puts the shot in Germany (c.1930).

Eric Sigward with Linda Muller (1957, both age 11).

Hans Sigward and Angela.
He served as athletic director of his own gymnasium.
She had three M.A.'s and practiced social work (1958).

**My sister Ellen while a student
at Hunter High School (1958).**

**Vincent and Maria Cosumano,
my grandparents (c. 1958).**

1966 Harvard heavyweight crew at EARC Sprints, Worcester, Massachusetts. The 1st place finish brings elation. We had an undefeated season and upstream record against Yale. (L–R) Paul Hoffman, Clint Allen, Brian Clemow, Andy Larkin, Curt Canning, Eric Sigward, Jacques Fiechter, Ian Gardiner, Jim Tew.

**Eric Sigward with legendary Harvard
crew coach, Harry Parker (1967).**

**Art Evans and Eric Sigward spare for the 1967 Pan American
Games. Evans stroked the Olympic eight next year.**

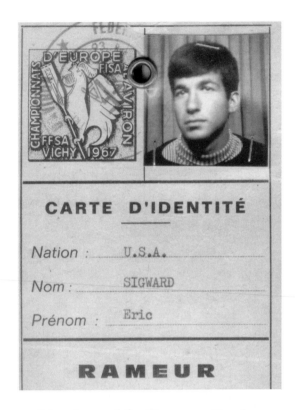

**Identity card for European Rowing
Championships, Vichy, France (1967).**

Art Evans and Eric Sigward train for the U.S. Rowing Team (1967).

Judith Bruce — tall, sweet and devastatingly intelligent (1968).

Eric Sigward and roomate Richard Grossman (May 1968).

**Graduation Day 1968 with (L-R) John Crocker,
Tom Ireland, Peter Schandorff, Eric Sigward.**

Eric Sigward in Trinity College Great Court with best friends John McKinnon and Johanna Andersen (October 1968).

Eric Sigward in festive attire at Trinity College (fall 1968).

Eric Sigward with Frazetta art poster of Conan the Barbarian and an oar which represents championship in the Clinker Fours (fall 1968).

Rowing to victory on the Cam river, the first and third Trinity College clinker four. (L–R) C. R. Harrison, A. I. Morley-Fletcher, Eric Sigward, M. F. Watts-Farmer, J. F. S. Hervey-Bathurst (1968).

(L-R) John McKinnon, and John S. Knight III in Marrakesh, Morocco (April 1969).

Eric Sigward in Trinity College Fellows Garden after the May Ball (June 1969).

Eric Sigward in front of his residence for second year at Cambridge, posing with Nehru Jacket (July 1969).

Mudi and Eric visit the boat tent at Henley (July 1969).

Night ride in Cambridge (October 1969).
Knitted hat and 6-foot scarf by Mudi.
I bought the handmade leather coat in Florence.

Eric Sigward on the Trinity College backs (spring 1970).

Eric Sigward back at home in New York City, donning handmade suit from Chelsea, London (June 1970).

Hippie friends in New York. (L-R) Unknown, Alan, Karen Hawes, and two-time Olympic oarsman, Cleve Livingston (1970).

Teacher, Mr. William R. Clinton, and son Billy with Dante on his T-shirt (1986).

Coach Eric Sigward and Stanford freshmen crew (June 1971).

**New convert to Christianity waves from
Peninsula Bible Church (spring 1972).**

With Professor Cornelius Van Til (June 1981).

CHAPTER 6: MUDI

And she was smooth and full as if
one gush of life had washed her,
or as if a sleep lay on her eyelid,
easier to sweep than bee from daisy.
— Beddoe 's Pygmalion

For some people blue eyes always suggest a cold, steely, northern aloofness. Mudi's, on the other hand, always seemed to stare into the warmth of some campfire. She became for me a warm, liquid color, like gold, glowing in my presence. As we loved with wine, and firesides, and kisses I used to think, "Will this one be the last? Have I found the ultimate love that will satisfy me? Is this home, and has the fickle dancing from girlfriend to girlfriend voluntarily come to an end?" Certainly Mudi's beauty held me entranced for one full year; but at the end of that time, passion for the infinite called me again, and I left her to pursue another dream.

Letter to Gil Eisenberg
October 23, 1968
Trinity College, Cambridge

Dear Gil,

Have no fear that your letters will depress me. I appreciate even your most morose letters. I suspect that you often have the feeling which I so readily experience — to say screw the whole thing and go find joy in the gentle petals of the lotus blossom off in the misty primal recesses of your own heart.

By the way, the fog here is otherworldly.

Apparently there is a stream of air that runs through Siberia, the North Sea, and Cambridge. The fog brings with it a soul-chilling supernatural cold. It seems that even the stones of the buildings brace themselves against the witch-weather. At times like these I trudge by gentle brontosauruses eating in the swampy Cam, wander by the baronial halls that seem to wail from centuries of persistent torture.

The girlfriend I have found here is splendid, certainly the woman for some Norseman such as Eric Sigward. She is the first person I have ever met to whom the name sounds familiar. Generally people think I have said something like Edgeward Seasick or Airwick Seaweed. She is very beautiful with golden hair and milky complexion. She also plays the same game of love with infuriating skill. I say, "You certainly must be the most beautiful girl in the world," and she answers, "Yes, indeed, I know." I say "I missed you very much, did you miss me?" She says with a perfect smile, "Why, no, of course not."

I am rowing frequently now, especially since I am in the middle of a four-day race schedule. My boat has utterly demolished two other boats so far, and Mudi coos when I return to the dock from the water, shrug my shoulders, and ask, "What did you expect?"

She, purring, "Yes, of course."

I met Prince Charles last week. He is very nice, in fact better than most, but I suppose he's required to be that. He's very straight and does everything by protocol. I don't know whether he's bothered by the restrictions placed on his life, but I really think someone his age could have a little more flamboyance; but the English are so reserved. They turn white and throw up mothballs if you talk about fighting the system. Charles had this little sexy blonde who now comes around looking for handouts, or love, or spontaneity, or whatever she's not getting from elsewhere.

Well, must sleep for very tough race on the morrow.

Eric

Within a month of meeting Mudi, I formally broke my relationship with Judy by letter; and Judy replied from Beirut

Letter from Judy Bruce
November 24, 1968
Beirut, Lebanon

Dear Eric,

I have spent a week deciding what to write you. Your letter was chilling. What I mean by a future is not of a romantic nature — that was finished in Rome — but of a communicative nature.

I know you're not one to have old girls as friends. I suspect that letters like this one mirrors the schizophrenia of our relationship: one is rapturous and nostalgic — the other, brutal and curt.

I am happy and very busy with study of Arabic working for a magazine, teaching English; and most promising, a special project with the UN that could become permanent if positions open up.

The men here are an assorted lot, but almost all universally tied to rigid forms of deportment. They are a bit dull with notable exceptions.

I feel very independent, and have managed to adjust to living alone in a beautiful apartment I decorated ME style.

I hope sometime you think I will 'understand' and write in more detail.

That's all,
Yours,
Judy

I spent my first year at Trinity enjoying every Epicurean luxury. The Trinity wine cellar provided excellent vintages. I rowed in the old style for pleasure and comradeship, and was no longer tortured by the unreachable goals I had faced at Harvard. James Hervey-Bathurst became a constant companion at the Trinity 1st & 3rd Boathouse. A year later, James assembled some friends and drove his family Land Rover into the Atlas Mountains of Morocco for a trip. While it was rumored that Harvard coach, Harry Parker, did not even eat coffee ice cream, we drank ale and lemon soda from the boathouse bar, a fixture that did not exist at Harvard. We even had a genuine Rock 'n 'Roll boathouse dance one winter. James lived in a nineteenth century castle in Herefordshire, and had a passion for steam engines which he visited all over the Continent. Eastnor Castle was on the border of Wales and surrounded by lovely country. James extended hospitality to Mudi and myself the summer of 1969 and the photographs of Mudi in this book are from his collection. During the Christmas vacation I went skiing in Austria and spent the holidays in Denmark. In the spring I purchased a 650-cc BSA and drove to Morocco.

Insofar as career plans went, I thought I would enter international banking or a social service organization like the UN. I read economics and sociology at Cambridge to complement the other social sciences I had studied at Harvard. I thought that by joining the psychology and anthropology that I had studied at Harvard with economics and sociology at Cambridge I would get an accurate understanding of human behavior.

Two things were apparent in my study of economics. First, there was the so-called quantitative sphere that attempted to measure causes and effects, *all other things being equal*. For instance, what is the effect on the price of steel when people demand greater quantities of it? Usually the price will go up when demand is increased, *all other things being equal* — that is, assuming that there have been no new discoveries of ore, or improvements of processes, etc. The simple counting of causes and effects amounted to the quantitative sphere of economics. Secondly, there was a moral sphere where economists tried to decide just what should be done with the data they have accumulated. For instance, should a few rich people own and control most of a region's steel?

The leap from the quantitative to the moral sphere was impossible for me, and it seemed equally impossible for all the economists I read. How could anyone dictate what should be, and on what basis? On the other hand, what possible use could data have apart from an understanding of what should be done with it? Who could unite facts and morals? And if no one could, then the exercises we played with tables and theories were all black comedy with no significance. I would have to play my role on the Cambridge stage as a fool and an idiot.

Because economics was a totally new field for me, I took the undergraduate course for two years. A week of study would include daily lectures, weekly meetings with tutors, and library work. Only at the end of a full two years would I take exams.

The English tutorial system of study was a major change from Harvard. Each week I prepared a paper on an assigned subject and submitted it to my tutor. During our meetings we discussed the subject, often over sherry, and critiqued my treatment of it. While the American concentration on classroom work produces large numbers of educated people, the English system seems geared to fewer, more scholarly types.

At the Christmas break, John and I went to Lech am Arlberg in Austria for two weeks of skiing, and then rode a train to Denmark for the holidays. Because Mudi was spending time with her family we stayed at Johanna's house, and I got to see very little of Mudi.

> Letter to Gil Eisenberg
> December 29, 1968
> Copenhagen

Dear Gil,

I traveled to Copenhagen with John McKinnon, another Harvard scholar at Cambridge, through Lech, Austria; Zurich, Switzerland; Cologne and

Hamburg, Germany. I wanted to see Copenhagen and Scandinavia in general in the winter. We had been invited to stay at Johanna's home. She is Mudi's best friend and John's amour. The four of us have spent most of the previous term together.

I came to Copenhagen expecting to see very little of Mudi. Because she is an *au pair* girl (an *au pair* girl lives with a family in a foreign country and helps with the housework), and gets only a fortnight vacation, she has to spend most of her time with her parents and with her Danish boyfriend at her summer house outside of Copenhagen. It has therefore been fairly difficult for me to see her while I have been here.

I think it was Gibran or Confucius or both who said something like "Love cannot be controlled or called, but live life so that it may come to you of itself." I'm trying, Gil, I'm trying.

No more dry thoughts from a dusty brain. It's a tale told by an idiot anyway. Love to you and warm joy for being alive and willing to fight for the next man's soul.

Eric

Before returning to Cambridge, John and I took a boat across the North Sea to Oslo, Norway. The art of Oslo, seeming to tug a forgotten heartstring, was otherworldly. We walked through the silent, snow-covered Vigeland Park to see sculptures of the stages and trials of life. The statues were monstrous in proportion and theme. In several of them men and women wrestled with huge reptiles and were seemingly defeated by the compelling force.

The paintings of Edvaard Munch struck a particularly relevant note, given my longing for Mudi. His overriding theme was the attraction of the sexes but their failure to understand each other's behavior. He showed a gape-faced staring man in front of a beautiful woman. His women were the most attractive I had seen since Botticelli. He virtually caressed and breathed with his figures, and gave them white skin that glowed and shimmered like northern lights.

When I returned to my rooms at Trinity I found a letter of consolation from Gil in which he warned me not to demand infinite love from another human being.

"You're not to make her into a mother image," he said. That summed up so much of my general tendency to want a one-way, infantile relationship with a woman.

> Excerpt from Gil Eisenberg
> January 3, 1969
> New York, New York

> Dear Eric,
> Life is not kind to any of us. Take this girl, Eric — take Mudi and accept her for what she is — you will be making a grave mistake if you do otherwise. She loves you the only way she knows how. Don't hate her if she can't give you love as you want it — rather understand that she gives only what she can. Don't allow your emotions to interfere with your relationship — Eric, if I buy you a gift — it's because I want to buy you a gift, not because I expect you to buy me a gift in return. So you must love her, of course, the only way you know how, but you must not expect her to love you the same way. And, she will give because she wants to. Be happy that you have somebody, that you have Mudi to walk in the rain with, that you have Mudi to hold. Don't look at others. Give to her, Eric, all the love you can — ask only that she appreciate it — not that she return everything you give — she can't and neither can you. I send you this poem.
> From the time you leave

Until the day you return
Nothing in this world —
Cherry-blossoms, maple leaves — Can seem
beautiful to me

Yasuro

In a subsequent letter I learned that Gil's girlfriend, Liz, had suddenly announced that she was marrying another man.

January 10, 1969
Trinity College

Dear Gil,

Forget Liz. She sounds like the archetype siren. I know you approached her because she held for you an infinite potential for suffering. You seem so much like Don Quixote who is always to be disappointed by reality, but always to be satisfied by his imaginative sensibility. This too is my problem: of reconciling reality with my emotional (artistic?) sensibility. You know, John Ruskin fell hopelessly in love with a nine-year-old girl. I am so depressed because I somehow feel that there is no woman for me. Perhaps this is the result of my strong and nurturing mother. Nevertheless, the male-female relationship seems so abysmally doomed to failure. John Keats got the shaft from Franny Brawn. Did you ever hear of Van Gogh? Well, with a little bit of black humor to keep our feet on the ground and a little bit of romance to keep our hearts in the clouds we should be able to work something out.

There is hope. I saw a picture of a cool motor-cycle girl crouched over her boyfriend who had been knocked down and was about to be beaten again by San Francisco U. cops. It's nice to be back in my room that has become my home. Seeing Mudi again has been wonderful. I was absolutely overwhelmed with joy to see her again, and I have promised myself to love her a la Eisenberg: love without unusual expectations.

Let there be joy, Gil; and let us save our souls together.

Eric

Mudi and I got along beautifully for the next term, and I loved her to tears. Though I might posture sternness, she broke through with a coo and a cuddle. I dreaded leaving her for an evening, yet alone forever.

In February, while gray clouds chilled Cambridge and icy winds blew through her streets, I bought a 650-cc BSA Thunderbolt motorcycle. Although two years old, it was still immaculate and I took it out to Grantchester to give Mudi a ride. Though the tour over flat East Anglian hills pleased me, Mudi's warm welcome pleased me more.

It seemed like an ideal relationship, and yet something was wrong. Although we shared intimacies, kisses, and endearing looks, and although we regretted every moment apart, we were not committed to marriage. We were in love, definitely, and belonged to one another in a real physical and emotional way; but something bright, shiny, and hard like steel was missing. There was no commitment of our persons, our lives. I could want her, hold her, kiss her and at the same time plan for further adventures in life without her. I could return to my room and coldly reflect on our joys or frustrations and on my own plans in the future apart from her. And this made for the roller coaster experience so many people have who say they are in love. One moment I was warm and she was in my arms, the next moment I was alone in my studies or rowing, and she was just a distant object of occasional gratification. If I called her and she was cold, it was unforgivable. How could she reject my great love and my need to be loved. I alternated between lover and self-pitying mother, whining that I deserved more for all my sacrifices.

It was alchemy. Into the cauldron had been thrown our youth, good looks, and education. In moonlight hours a golden hue appeared in the brew. Gold! We thought, but it was an unstable element and the hoped-for transformation did not occur. The ingredients returned to base materials. As yet the magical conversion was impossible, for we could not overcome our innate selfishness to be genuinely married and in true love.

At the end of winter term McKinnon bought a Norton motorcycle, and in mid-March we trekked to Marrakesh, Morocco. John would start three days behind me since he had studies to complete in Cambridge. We would rendezvous in Madrid and travel together from there.

A thousand chores needed attention before I went — laundry, haircut, letters, packing, and writing an article for the Trinity Review. When would I have time for Mudi? Not since the days when I cried at leaving my mother for summer camp had I felt the desperate sorrow of leaving someone.

To compound the dread, my senior Tutor told me I had not been working hard enough. Nevertheless, St. Patrick's Day 1969 found me on the ferry crossing from Dover to Calais with my motorcycle. I had irascibly departed from Cambridge that morning determined to make it to Dover despite the pouring rain. The last day with Mudi had been sublime. We glowed with such intensity that tears came to my eyes. I had told her that she should spend a week with me after the Henley Rowing Regatta but she was afraid of how this would affect her parents. I had told her to make a choice, told her that I wanted to be Number One.

That night I slept in Paris, and a day later traveled about 600 km south to Cahors where I got caught in a downpour. In the early afternoon of March 20th I saw the sun for the first time since England. The clouds parted at the Spanish border, revealing the snow-capped Pyrenees. The colors of the Spanish landscape were the richest and most iridescent I had seen. Spring had brought lush green and flowers, and as I passed through the fields I could smell their sweetness.

Barcelona was fascinating, as Oslo was fascinating. The

subterranean, biological-ooze architecture of Gaudi caught me for a few days. Then it was on to Madrid, which offered all that New York does, including overpricing, impersonal treatment, high-powered businesses, and anonymity. American Express held untold joy: a letter from Mudi, saying she missed me; a telegram from McKinnon saying he was on his way; and a note from a Cambridge and Harvard buddy, Joe Kanon, indicating time of a possible meeting in Marrakesh.

> Letter from Mudi
> March 18, 1969
> Grantchester, England

Dear Eric,

> Thank you so much for your postcard. I'm glad to hear that you have started but my God what a weather! I felt so sorry for you yesterday morning and I went around the whole day, thinking you would phone me and tell that you would not leave until it was nice outside. But I'm glad that you have taken off for then I can start looking forward to your return. AND I DO LOOK FORWARD TO SEEING YOU AGAIN! I miss you so much. I really had not thought that it would be that bad, but it is and it has already started, how will it not be later? Ugh.

> My English is bad and my spelling hopeless: I'm fed up with it! Forgive me and just pretend that all the mistakes are not there.

> Miss you.

> Love and kiss,
> Mudi

I left Madrid alone, having waited three days for McKinnon without luck; and after a short ride south, caught sight of the

Toledo skyline. I did my obligatory sightseeing there, most of which centered around El Greco.

A day later I drove from Toledo to Malaga and stopped in Granada to see the Alhambra. Once a cool summer palace for sultans, the Alhambra sits on a cloud-high perch over a pleasant valley. The white snows of neighboring mountains provide water; and the sun sets it its windows, throwing pink and red highlights onto elaborate filigreed stucco. In adjacent cliffs, gypsies still hold evening flamenco dances.

The ride from Granada to Malaga twists through the lower reaches of the Sierra Nevadas. The precipitous ledges, the hovering fog, and the pastel-red sunset make the journey magical. El Greco certainly derived his colors and elongations from the enchanted scenery of the south. The cliffs drop so suddenly to the sea that one corkscrews down the mountain to the sea in an instant. Literally, one must drive in circles to come off the mountainside.

April 1st I ferried across the Straight of Gibraltar to Tangiers. Morocco is so suddenly different from Spain that I found myself keenly concentrating on each person, his smallest moves, and his deepest motivation. From the moment I disembarked, the unexpected and dreamlike occurred. A swarthy Moroccan, speaking good American slang, approached me.

"Are you Eric?"

"Why, yes'?"

"Groovy, baby" he said. "A cat named John came through yesterday, he was looking for you, said you were on a blue motorcycle, said you were a far-out cat."

"Where is he?"

"Hotel Tahiti, Rue Michel Ange'; you gonna be there?"

"I think I will."

"Groovy baby, I'll catch you later."

I trusted him for his consideration in giving me the information, and learned later of his work as a dock hustler and contact for *kief*, the Moroccan grass.

Like the jungles of Tennessee Williams, Tangiers was a place of primitive passions and activities. The ride from the dock to the hotel was bizarre. All along the way haggard and debased people darted in front of the motorcycle and screamed offers for help. Beggars in town sat in rows on special streets. The rest of my stay in Tangiers offered further contrasts. The family resident in the hotel sat, cooked, and ate on the floor. A 125-dirham robe could be had for 25. No one was to be trusted; the lowest price was robbery; one feared dysentery, malaria, hepatitis, etc., etc. The disfigured children were so much uglier because of their hardened disingenuousness.

I looked on the rest of my stay in Morocco as a mixed blessing, feeling that the sights I was about to see spelled death for the civilized life I had always considered to be the only and real one. I drove to Marrakesh through biblical gardens and landscapes, smelling jasmine, mint, saffron, mocha, and oranges. After ten hours I saw the first camel caravan and soon arrived in Marrakesh. I parked the blue bike in the center of town and had coffee. Fifteen minutes later McKinnon saw the machine and found me. We hugged and I noticed a bright flush of embarrassed love come to his face.

John was with two friends from England, John Knight and Scott Smith; and all four of us slept and smoked *kief* in the bus station hotel that overlooked the medina, or open square. Below us we could see, hear, and smell the snake charmers, barbecues, beggars and cripples. Children were valueless and hated by older people because they threatened the older beggars' business.

Since John's motorcycle had collapsed in Tours, France, he had ridden down to Morocco with his friends. This accounted for his delay in Madrid. We agreed to ride double on my bike back as far as Tours where he would obtain his repaired bike.

After three days in Marrakesh, John and I drove back to Tangiers where I got bombed on hash and marijuana flowers.

On the return journey through Madrid I received another letter from Mudi.

Letter from Mudi
April 5, 1969
Grantchester, England

Dear Eric,

How I hoped to get a card from you this morning, saying when you would return, but no. I'm still kept in suspense (if you say so) and I miss you. I have never in my whole life waited for someone as I'm waiting now for you. You better hurry back or there will be great trouble.

Love,
Mudi
Kiss to you.

Four days and two thousand miles later McKinnon and I pulled into Cambridge with a pound of *kief* in our pockets. Exhausted and filthy we arrived at Mudi's house, and I saw an excited Mudi come through the kitchen door, skin white, a little plumper, beaming with love. That night total collapse took me, and I sent Mudi home from my rooms in a taxi. This brought me home on April 13, approximately four weeks after departure. I had traveled 4700 miles without a mechanical failure or serious complaint about the motorcycle. I now wished only to be alone and warm with her.

At Harvard, University Hall had been occupied by demonstrating students; police with nightsticks had removed the protestors. Tom Ireland was engaged in mobile street tactics against the Stanford Research Institute in California. And I was in a hashish stupor.

CHAPTER 7: THE SUMMER OF '69

Across the margent of the world I fled,
And troubled the gold gateways of the stars.
— Francis Thompson, *The Hound of Heaven*

Having read Tom Wolfe's *Electric Cool-Aid Acid Test* the spring of '69, I felt I had a new handbook to life, complete with how to talk, what to think, and what to ingest. "Neither accept nor deny, go with the flow." "Grok?" "Now is the moment." "Are you on the bus?" Phrases like these embodied the cryptic philosophy of the psychedelic world. Ken Kesey had explored a new world of drugs, and in particular LSD with an entourage of friends called 'The "Merry Pranksters." Together they had driven a psychedelically painted bus from California, across the United States, and back again. Along the way they spread drugs, partied, and filmed the occurrences. The sheer gusto of their lives fascinated me, and fired my imagination. Before finishing the book I had resolved to alter my lifestyle to accord with Wolfe's descriptions of sex and drugs among the Merry Pranksters. April, McKinnon told Johanna about Rosemary, the girl he eventually married. There was no chance, however, that I would leave Mudi. I would be lonely for the rest of my life if I did. The joy of Mudi's company made time an enemy. Each of our moments should have been an impressionistic painting. I brought Mudi home one night and stood at her doorstep across the road from the Granchester church giving thanks to God for the beauty I felt that moment. On arrival back in Cambridge I almost forgot the experience as I got stoned on hash. The past ceased to exist and I was in the moment.

It was an easy slide from the pleasures of club life, world travel, and an overindulged fantasy life into the exotic world of drugs. Like the fabled fruit of Eden, drugs offered what promised to be wonderful, exciting, and expanding; but turned out to be shameful, disastrous, and disappointing. Two signs appeared at this time that pointed to a deteriorating lifestyle. First, I used the hip argot and slang readily to describe my activities and feelings; and secondly, I began to see my relationship with Mudi as an aesthetic experience. What was pleasing, sensual, or exciting was justifiable; and in a small but expanding way Mudi was becoming a stepping stone for my own wanderlust. But I could not then see the road I was following, and one more great joy lay in store for me and Mudi — the Trinity College May Ball, held in June.

Diary:

June 11, 1969

I feel some compassion with Keats' feeling of melancholy over passing beauty, "Never seemed it so rich to die." The last two days have been so unrelentingly joyous that I am now stirred with sadness and despair that the future holds only comparative disappointments.

Monday was sunny and I busied myself with small preparations for the giant evening. I was up at ten after a previous night's psychedelic prancing at Fiona Smith-Russel's party, had lunch at Trinity, then bought a pair of blue sunglasses for Mudi as a May Ball present. The familiar road to Grantchester was so much more lovely in the bright sunlight — rich green of the Trinity cricket grounds, warm smell of cut hay waiting to be baled, dip and accelerate around the corners, zip into the driveway of Connor's Grove. There stands Mudi, combing and sifting her damp hair in the sun. She wears a blue play dress with a low neckline. Smiles, kisses, rush.

We shop in the market for party favors: food,

presents, balloons. Mudi gives me a large mother-of-pearl shell for which I have longed. We go punting, glowing at each other, not walking, floating. She glows as we glide among the trees, passing through bright and shady spots. After punting we go to my rooms. I shave while Mudi sleeps.

Then we both dressed in evening wear, and went by motorcycle to a cocktail party in the Magdalene Fellow's garden. Mudi wore an orange nylon pantsuit. Her waist was tied with gold rings. She wore blue eye shadow and long earrings made of gold disks.

The drink at Magdalene was stronger than we had expected, and after two rounds we were laughing and falling over each other. We then met Jake and Cindy Ellis, and headed back to my rooms for an early dinner.

At eleven P.M. we left the table to enter upon the ball that people attend from distant cities like New York, Rome, Copenhagen, Paris, and Geneva. Two spotlights illuminated New Court's giant chestnut tree and the pink blossoms shined color on all the walls. Couples were converging from every direction, dressed in finest clothes — girls with long dresses and coiffeured hair, men in long black mourning coats. All of us moved toward the entrance of Neville's Court where porters checked admission tickets. Spotlights, too, illuminated Neville's Court. The colonnades had been turned into areas for drinking and dancing. Music blared everywhere. Smiling people in shining clothes greeted one another and passed on to new friends. At the far end of the court, near the Old Kitchen, a bandstand had been erected for performers.

Before our second dinner at eleven-thirty, we strolled out of Neville's Court onto the Backs. Like a market in Marrakesh, the backs were alight with glowing braziers around which couples could be seen warming themselves, kissing, talking — silhouetted or illuminated by the glowing fires. Their moving shadows were thrown up against the walls of the College. And on the far side of the river to the left of the bridge, a large fire lit up the backs with its warmth. Every willow was alight like a Christmas tree with colored bulbs. And with the light of the colored braziers, the whole of the Backs was enchanted.

On the far side was a large circus tent to which we walked, covered by colored awnings all the way. In the tent, an African band boinked and bonked on steel drums as otherwise staid couples were dancing with ecstatic energy.

Our dinner of *poulet chasseuse* was a disappointment, but it was pleasant to see the Hall sparkling with candles, silver, and jewels. Too soon, however, the effect of three bottles of champagne became evident. At one-thirty, Mudi and I could stand no more, and we retired for two hours.

The last notes of Geno Washington and his Ramjets awakened us as he belted out his last soul-electric song. Up again to see what was happening, we came upon a vaguely dismal scene. The morning had come, and the lights no longer shone with their former brilliance. Papers and cups blew over the trampled lawns and couples staggered from the lavatories. However, much of the fun for Mudi and me had just begun. We listened to the Irish Guard Bagpipers, danced, and eventually attended Churchill's Ball.

At six, fourteen of us had breakfast at the Plough Pub next to the Cam; and at eight we drove to Trinity in an open-backed lorry, dropping couples along the way. Fatigue had caught up with us, and there was no more to enjoy in that physical state.

Mudi and I awoke at noon and motorcycled to Ely for lunch. We spent the day touring the Ely Cathedral and walking in the Trinity Fellows Garden. Evening we went to John's room for a cocktail party, after which I drove Mudi home. The ride home was short, but both of us had been gripped by the sense of nostalgia about the previous day — how we had loved it and each other, how I wanted it to be May Ball 1970. In so many ways this Ball represents the height of my youth, my aesthetic appreciativeness, my love for a girl, my social achievement. Now the future seems to pall by comparison to this night. The future holds worries about packing, rowing, moving — and most perturbing of all — Mudi's going.

July 2, 1969 the *Daily Mail* had a cover story of the investiture of Charles as Prince of Wales at Caernarvon Castle. Page three covered the Henley Royal Regatta, with a large picture of a young Harvard, myself, kissing his eternal damsel by the sweetly flowing Thames. We lost a close race to Nereus of Holland who went on to win the Ladies Plate. After the regatta Mudi and I toured the English countryside and ten days later I put Mudi on the boat for Denmark. We cried at the pier, but I realized there was no point in making a public scene. And so I sent her up the gangplank, and went back to the car where I collapsed in tears. Gil sent us a seventh-century poem.

How will you manage
To cross alone
The autumn mountain
Which was so hard to get across
Even when we went the two of us together.

Letter to Gil Eisenberg
July 14, 1969
London, England

Dear Gil,

As always, your letters are full of compassion and human understanding. The poem you sent to me and Mudi was beautiful and appropriate. I don't know how I shall get along without her. I put her on the boat the day before yesterday and we collapsed in each other's arms, sobbing and weeping. I really collapsed, Gil. I couldn't see for an hour after she left. Oh, God, I was sad, but now I am better because I am firm in my conviction that I shall see her again soon and that eventually we shall get married. How strange to think in those terms, but it is the only thing I can do — must do, because I *must* be with her; and I will be sad the rest of my life if I don't keep her.

I shall be c/o American Express, Paris, France until July 23. Write there. Or until July 30 – c/o Ritz Carlton Hotel, Cannes, France.

I feel better now that I have written you. Oh, Gil, life has become so simplified this year. No neuroses, no undefined motives. So boldly simplified.

Eric

In my heart, I had promised to marry Mudi, and I had even given here a ring before she left; but my word was air. Ignorance, fear, and cowardice were in fact stronger forces than my romantic love for Mudi. First of all, the path my parents had taken did not provide a hopeful trajectory for our love. I could only foresee irreconcilable selfishness and ultimate failure. Secondly, both laziness and innate perversity militated against any selfless acts of courage. Within the dream world of my scholarship, Mudi was entirely loveable; but I was incapable at that time of taking realistic measures towards marriage. Perhaps our affair had been doomed from the start, and had been launched on altogether the wrong terms. Perhaps the alchemical transformation was impossible and better left undone rather than done tragically. This I know — that my affair with Mudi marked forever the end of innocence. What replaced her is too sad to describe fully.

July 19, 1969 Neil Armstrong set foot on the moon, and I watched it from Veronique's Paris apartment on my way to Crete. I had just had lunch with Veronique and Irene, her existential friend.

"What's wrong," I had asked Irene, noticing her despondency.

'Life," she replied.

"Oh, yes," I cheerfully complied, "no love?"

"Nobody cares, nobody," Irene concluded.

That night I found Irene's clothing strewn over the apartment, the bathroom door locked, and the bathroom light on. "Suicide," I felt surely, and proceeded to kick a hole in the door to get Irene. Apparently the door was only jammed and Irene had been sloppy rather than suicidal because there was no Irene in the tub as I had expected and I was left with a story of mock-heroics.

From Paris I planned to ride south through France to Cannes, and then through Italy to Rome where I would rendezvous with Joe Kanon, the friend from Trinity and Harvard. We planned to ride double to Brindisi, and catch a boat to Corfu. I hoped to catch up with the hip crowd in Crete — members of the dropout generation like those I had met in Marrakesh and on the Spanish Steps of Rome. It would not be hard to identify them: middle-class, educated, disillusioned and committed to the psychedelic experience. I justified interest in drugs because I had found no rationale for behavior in either sports or the social sciences. Without an ultimate reason for behavior, life could only be seen as theatre of the absurd. At least those who ingested drugs did not pretend to be reasonable or moral. Instead, they honestly acted out their absurd philosophy of rebellion.

I had friends, studies, rowing and a lovely fiancée waiting in Denmark: but I searched for a sublime madness. Like the Fool in the Tarot deck, I was about to walk off a cliff; and Cannes brought me one step closer to the abyss.

July 30, 1969
Ritz Carlton
Cannes

Dear Gil,

I am in one of those nervous frenetic, claustro-phobic moods that make me hyperactive and generally restive. Perhaps it is the coffee or bad comedown from the dope. Anyway, I am here in Cannes, safe and alive in the hands of the parents of a great friend from NY. They have been like second parents to me since I was eleven, and now they are putting me up in this elegant hotel for a week's vacation of sun and surf.

I read Robert Heinlein's *Stranger in a Strange Land,* sci-fi about a Martian who comes to earth. Remarkable parallels to drug culture — a Christ story.

Good vocabulary: "To Grok" is to drink in, immerse oneself in, total absorption-emulsion. You'll grok the book.

Hoping you are reaching fullness. I am only an egg.

Eric

In addition, I received a letter from Mudi, confirming our engagement.

Letter from Mudi
July 19, 1969
Copenhagen

Dear Eric,

Oh, thank you for calling me. I was so happy to hear your voice; tears were streaming out of my eyes and my heart was beating so loudly that I could hardly hear you. It was so good to talk to you; but I didn't really tell you how much I care for you, but I do, I do.

By the way, you can consider yourself engaged to be married to Miss Mudi Hellberg.

Thank you. Hey. Hey. It's terrible, I'm tying you hands and feet, but I cannot help it because I do not want to lose you. I want to be yours and be with you always. So if we just go on loving each other as we do now then everything will be all right.

I love you, too, very much.

Mudi

I met Joe on the Spanish Steps in Rome, Joe's senior thesis on Henry James had been recognized by the Harvard English Department as the best submitted that year. Having been introduced to him at Trinity, I was greatly impressed by his thorough knowledge of English. From Rome, Joe and I went south to Sorrento, took another excursion to the Blue Grotto, and then crossed the ankle of Italy to Brindisi and the boat for Corfu. We traversed the Adriatic by night, and in the morning haze we beheld the dark humps of Corfu and several smaller Greek isles.

We slept for one week on a Corfu beach, ate salads in the shade of cafes, and at night smoked grass and looked at the stars. In the afternoons we swam in the fairest blue water I have ever seen.

A short boat ride and a very hot, dusty road took us to Delphi, "The Navel of the Earth," and the site of the ancient oracle. It was so hot in Delphi that Joe and I could drink water until we were bloated, and be thirsty again in half an hour. In fact, we spent much of our time in Greece going from store to store ordering Tam-Tam, a Greek imitation of Coca-Cola.

In Athens, I found an anxious letter from Mudi.

Letter from Mudi
July 30, 1969
Copenhagen

My Dear Eric,

I've just returned from Jutland and what did I find in the hall? Two letters from you! Eric, it was so beautiful to hear from you though your letter frightened me a little. I'm not quite able to explain why it did, maybe because of all your talk about us and sex, and us being free. You know though I've always tried not to show you that I was jealous, I have been more than once and I'm sure to be again. And I don't want you to be with somebody else. I know that it is silly of me to be in that way. I want you to be free at the same time. Do you understand what I mean? I don't want to make love with or just be near and kiss another man, not only because I want to be faithful to you but also because if I start an affair with somebody else I'll get so much involved and I'll have trouble getting out of it again.

Eric I send you all my love and hopes,

Kiss,
Mudi

From Athens Joe and I decided to take a boat to Crete, and in thirteen hours we were standing in the busy town of Heraklion. The Cretan terrain, like much of Greece, is a series of rugged mountain ranges surrounding fertile valleys. The ruins of ancient Phaestos, for instance, sits on a high table overlooking a broad green valley. This kind of terrain has inevitably produced communities that are socially and economically isolated from one another; and consequently, the people of Greece are very free and fiercely individualistic. The islanders were perpetually generous and happy in '69, even though an oppressive military regime was governing in Athens.

Joe and I drove through the wonder of the Cretan landscape on the way south. First there was a low valley with a stream and grapes on the hillsides. Then we rose into hot, dry mountains — cactus, stone, brush, and dust. In the distance we could see the light blue sea. We descended into another valley, crossed it, and climbed again into the hills. On a flat terrace sat the ruins of Phaestos. The road descended again through vineyards and dust, rose again into hills; and a vast, sweeping S-curve took us down to the sea and Matala.

From afar it looked like a small horseshoe cove. The left and right bends of the horseshoe were sandstone cliffs that slanted into the sea. A mile off in the deep, a purple mountain rose out of the water. Joe and I sat in the town cafe to survey the cove. The town of Matala, on the east side of the horseshoe, was a fishing village, constructed of small lime-washed houses. On the west side of the cove holes were visible in the sandstone cliff — doors and windows to the caves of Matala. The caves, we learned, had been tombs once and later the homes of lepers. These explanations seemed feasible since the caves were both decorative and functional. Their darkness and coolness gave them a monastic peacefulness; and since they had been carved by man and not by water, they were entirely dry and habitable.

During our two weeks in the caves, we met Pat, a Ph.D. candidate in philosophy from Pennsylvania, and her Great Dane, Cerberus; two French girls from the Sorbonne; Madge, a recluse from New Jersey; Rico, an Italian poet; and Jan, a drug tramp from Holland. It could have been any one of a number of urban graduate schools. There was, however, one very obvious difference between these people and any we had previously seen.

Joe and I realized their distinctiveness on our first evening in Matala. In the gathering dusk, inhabitants from the caves were walking across the beach towards the cafe. The young people were buzzing with conversation about places seen, books, philosophical insights, and of course, drugs. In front of the cafe, on the beach, an octagonal concrete platform had been built and surmounted by several loudspeakers. With dinner completed, and the benevolent cool of night upon us, the cafe music was switched on.

"I AM THE LORD GOD OF HELLFIRE, AND I COME TO BRING YOU FIRE!" As this music filled our ears, a score of people left their tables to dance on the platform. Arthur Brown sang his song. "FIRE, FIRE, FIRE."

The music took us by surprise, but as we watched the dancers, another fact intrigued us. Hardly anyone was dancing with anyone else. Boys danced with boys, girls danced with girls, most danced alone and freely acted out their imaginations. A circle might form of all holding hands, rush towards the center with a shout, then dissolve. Or Jan, barefooted and pony-tailed, might dance in the center of the ring as all danced around him. When the music stopped, people kept dancing, shaking, jittering in place like disconnected live wires until the next song. I had seen people dance wildly, but never without music. What was going on invisibly in their heads was as powerful as the audible music.

Joe looked at me. "I've never seen dancing like this, this is another world," he said.

"Dope, Joe."

"But what kind of dope? This sort of thing doesn't happen on grass."

"It's pills of some sort, probably acid."

"What do you want to do?"

"I think if it's acid, it's going to change our lives. That's what happened with Kesey." I gave Joe my opinions since neither of us had tried hard drugs at that time. "Let's find out what they're taking, Joe."

We asked Jan, who seemed to be the immediate trip guide

and authority on drugs, and found that the kids of Matala were using two readily available Greek medicines for their trips. At least it wasn't LSD, we thought, and so we would be protected in some measure. By the next evening we had consumed several bottles of the local cough medicine and were dancing ecstatically on the shores of great Ulysses.

The ingestion of pills marked an advance in our use of drugs. First, the leap from grass to medicines meant that we were experiencing the prolonged effects that only stronger doses of drugs could give. And secondly, we were philosophically opened for a dramatic change in lifestyle. No one who planned to spend twelve hours of a day in euphoric separation from reality could expect to study deeply, hold a usual job, or maintain the same friends. The pursuit of the drug experience necessarily required a drop from traditional society, and the establishment of a drug culture to replace it.

Why would anyone hazard these changes? To an extent the answer lay in what the drugs appeared to promise. The seductiveness of drugs lay largely in the belief that they would open realms of the mind ordinarily inaccessible and that these realms would be rich, vast, intricate and awesome. I was attracted by the potentialities drugs seemed to offer — understanding of self, expanded perception, social utopia and religious insight. In particular, the transcendental philosophies and experiences of tripping intrigued me.

One night in Matala I was convinced that I myself had reached transcendental heights of insight and rapture. I felt a oneness with all things and a pantheistic awe for God. But the deficiency of personality or morality in the euphoric state posed a problem that only Homer could then answer. Having achieved the elevated consciousness one night, and having proclaimed to myself, "This is it," I could not see any possible distinctions between good and evil, or worse, between the natural objects around me and Me! It was all experientially — and thus I thought, absolutely — one. The perverted logic of a Manson and the free love of the flower children were all one.

But if all were one, then there was no possible excuse for ever coming down off drugs. I was compelled by philosophy to addiction. What is more, there was no excuse for ever communicating anything again, not even to Mudi or my mother.

In fact there was no excuse for me to ever leave that blissful isle. Sickening terror took hold of my soul, for I was logically a transcendent being and belonged to no one but the sea, the stars and the moon; and the cold impersonality of this realization made me cry out in childlike fear. Bummer!

Here I must give eternal thanks to Homer because I remembered that Odysseus had fled from the land of the Lotus-Eaters. Likewise, he had been tied to the mast as they sailed past the Sirens. He had subdued and abandoned Circe's supernatural love, and had pined for home even in the arms of a nymph, Calypso. Man, it seemed, was not made for these pleasures; he chooses the homely and prosaic when he is offered the cold infinite. On the basis of Odysseus's preference for his aged wife over all else, I left our catacomb the next morning for good.

I was fighting my way back to finitude and personality — fighting north through Greece and Yugoslavia, driving hard to get to Mudi: Athens, heat, Larisa, mechanical trouble, Thessaloniki, cool Skopje, Zagreb, Ljubljana and collapse. The bike blew a bolt through the crankcase and stopped for good. Rather than ship it to England for repairs, we abandoned it in the mountains near Ljubljana and caught a bus to Klagenfurt, Austria.

Joe, who had had enough motorcycling, joyfully boarded a train in Klagenfurt bound for London. I stayed behind to watch the European Rowing Championships in Klagenfurt, and after the races took a plane with the Danish crew to Copenhagen.

For the next ten days, Mudi and I tried to deny what was evident. "Close your eyes with holy dread, for he on honeydew hath fed, and drunk the milk of paradise." Coleridge's poem described my change from contented lover to drug freak. I had become a restless, disinterested stranger to Mudi, prowling the streets of Copenhagen for dope and friends in the drug culture.

When I returned to Cambridge, I wrote Mudi to explain that I was committed to the drug experience, and I did not think she could understand.

> Letter from Mudi
> October 6, 1969
> Copenhagen

Dear Eric,

Today a year ago we met each other; it has been a year of joy, pleasure and happiness but now that part is over. I can never thank you enough for what you've been to me and I'll always remember you.

(She went on to say she was furious at my attitude, that I was the most selfish man she had ever met, that I should find another dumb blonde; and she had seen a new side of me. In addition, her old boyfriend was fated for her.)

I'm sorry, Eric, forgive me, please. Don't be too hard on me just forget me.

Thank you for everything.

Mudi

Eric, I'm terribly sorry. Do forgive me.

I returned to Cambridge from Copenhagen thinking I would go on living as usual, engaging in casual relationships and taking drugs for fun. My expectations could not have been more wrong. Despite affectations to the contrary, I had committed a sacrilege in abandoning Mudi and my conscience would feel an awesome weight of guilt. And what is more, leaping through the dimensional portals a heavier trip yet was coming down.

CHAPTER 8: OCCULTISM

Things fall apart; the centre cannot hold;
Mere anarchy is loosed upon the world,
The blood-dimmed tide is loosed, and everywhere
The ceremony of innocence is drowned
The best lack all conviction, while the worst
Are full of passionate intensity.
                    – Yeats, *The Second Coming*

Letter to Gil Eisenberg
October 10, 1969

Dear Gil,

This summer was apocalyptic for my thinking.
I took some drugs and a being that was asleep for
geological ages came awake, and being awake it is
likely to remain so for the infinite future. It's not
drugs though, it's the reaction, the changing of the
mind, and the realization that there are psychic realities of different planes just as there are genuses of a
species. And in many ways now it's not that I wish
to be different, I just will never be the same. And part
of never being the same is that I now know that there
are many realities. My mind still booms as I see the
world from many more eyes. It's so hard to stop
drug taking because nothing in the straight world
compares to it; and also, as I said, the experience is a
being awakened, not just a ten-hour effect.

Eric

I consider the drug experience to be highly subjective and the geography of the trip essentially unmappable. I was deceived in thinking that what I experienced artificially through drugs was especially real. Drugs, by suspending the normal outgoing activities of the mind, left an introspective residue in which there was no will, no logic, no morals, and no mental categories. This mere chaos of the dream world we called "high," "far out," or "awake." We were misinformed.

Towards the winter of 1969 I still had a large supply of *kief* from Morocco, and so a group of us smoked in my room several nights each week. I led a double life. I played the part of Harvard scholar and oarsman outwardly — trekking to classes, tutors, and rowing. Inwardly, however, I was experiencing the chaos of drugs and lust. A sense of guilt developed from the duality of lifestyle. In response to the division, I turned paranoid and schizophrenic. Severe depressions arose from the conflict; and perceiving I could not serve both God and Satan, I chose Satan.

The occult promised to be an answer to my human needs and an integration point for my experience with sex and drugs. First of all, sex without love was abhorrent and I was recoiling from physical encounters. I could no longer endure the persistent defrauding called free love. Fear, however, is no substitute for human warmth. How, then, could I overcome the paralyzing guilt and fear I associated with sex? I thought the answer lay in power and occult control.

Secondly, drugs played a part in driving me towards the occult. The profound images of the drug experience needed to be grouped, categorized and explained. The occult seemed to provide an integrating terminology for the loose aggregate of striking experiences. I'm no hero; I wanted power and insight to heal my fears and replace my ignorance.

I began a reflective search into the teachings of Aleister Crowley — mystical poet, novelist, mountain climber, and writer of books on magic (1875-1947). He had been educated at Trinity College and strove to assume the magician's mantle. Violently hostile to Christianity and the Christian God, he openly flaunted his practices as the messiah of a new aeon. Like famous occultists before him, he was credited with remarkable, if not miraculous powers. Not only his background at Trinity fascinated me, but also his apparent familiarity with the remote, terrible world of spirits and demons. Surely, I felt, the answer to my depressions lay in the spirit world. He had written shelves of seemingly scholarly work on the subject of magic; and as the prophet of a new astrological age, had shown that sex and drugs could be used ritually or magically.

The occult stimulates two responses in us: longing and loathing. With irrational, subconscious passion we are drawn towards the exotic symbols and paraphernalia of the occult; and at the same time we are repelled by their seediness, guilt and concealment. Somerset Maugham, who based *The Magician* on Aleister Crowley, said of their first encounter, "I hated him, he was a phony, but not that phony."

Diary
February 20, 1970

So much has happened since my last entry. Worlds have been rent and universes torn. I fear that my lust for experience has somehow dulled my sensitivity to people. Those who suffer sometimes tolerate weakness least in others. I have also found myself deeply involved in and committed to the drug culture. This past summer I dropped acid, lost my firm hold on the old reality — and since the mind has no amnesia, I have yet to take hold of some newer or firmer way of life. The awareness of the universe within me makes me want to realize fully my human potential. Unfortunately, internal travel is so lonely and all the monsters have to be defeated alone. I am still, from time to time, drawn up short with a pain in my heart and mind at the thought of Mudi. I loved her so completely that her memory shakes me terribly and threatens to reproach me for my firm purpose to experience what I know I must alone. How I wish she could have come, but there was no compromise.

And so now I am exploring the ancient texts of forgotten lore, seeking experience at any cost, investigating sword and sorcery, mediums, Eastern Religion and especially "Black Magick". On Aleister Crowley's recommendation, therefore, I begin my diary anew, this time to recount my voyages into the occult.

I have collected a fairly large supply of Crowleyana, but today for the first time I got the feeling of the evil I was pursuing. God and Satan wrestled for my soul. God won. But which of the two was God?

I bought the *Confessions of Aleister Crowley* at Bowes and Bowes bookshop. After the purchase, one of the salesmen approached me. "Are you interested in performing some Black Magick?" he asked.

"Yes."

"I can give you the names of some people in London who are still in the A.A., Crowley's cult."

"What do they do?" I asked.

"I can't say."

"Oh, *that's* occult."

"Yes, if you're interested."

"I am," I said, "what's your name?"

"Indra, it's Indian."

His face was sin-pocked, lethargic, almost doped. One tooth was cracked, or perhaps filed. I immediately thought that Black Magick (Crowley's spelling) must be for the ugly; and I envisioned perverse orgies, compromising my usual tastes and submitting to awful physical and psychological humiliations. 'Try everything,' Crowley said. Could I? I wondered. The feeling of evil crept over the mind I had kept so uncluttered by discomfiture. What are nameless evil and horror, motiveless malignity and such? I wonder.

One February afternoon when light snow covered the Cambridge commons, I was reading Crowley's *Magick* and came across the following paragraph:

> The magician must keep his concentration absolute during this ritual, lest he be infallibly possessed by a demon. Death may result in the form of epilepsy, apoplexy, or strangulation. Blood is required for this ritual: a chicken will do, but in all cases human sacrifice is most efficacious.

I had not dabbled long before realizing the impact of the magical path. Crowley had tossed off the statement about human sacrifice as though he were talking about margarine, butter or fat in a recipe. Having no morality myself, however, I was in no position to pass judgment on Crowley.

For several days in February, reports of supernatural happenings passed my way. A dear, warm friend at Trinity had read me portions of *Revelation* from the Bible. Another had described two dreams, and a third had a vision on acid. All included descriptions of golden streets, golden walls, jeweled towers and angels. And finally, my friend Giles had seen demons with long, tentacle-arms coming at him through the walls one night on an acid trip.

Early March I attended Nick Mander's birthday party at Giles' house in the country. The usual dancing and drug parley occupied the early part of the evening.

"Are you something out of my consciousness?" a friend asked.

"No, you're out of mine," I said. He flipped over a couch, laughing.

"That's right, that's right," he cried, seeing that there was as much sense to my comment as there was to his.

By that time, my heart was openly lustful. As the larger body of guests began to leave I embraced Audrey, a lithe girl, and we passionately kissed for several minutes. After she and the crowd had departed, Joe, Giles and I swallowed small violet-colored pills and sat listening to music, waiting for the LSD to take effect. I mused on Audrey, who had just left, with a sense of despair. Of course, I had enjoyed her warmth and love; but I could foresee only chaos and doom based on what I had done with Peta, Judy, and Mudi.

King Crimson was singing *Twenty-First Century Schizoid Man*, as the trip started. I began to breathe heavily, willfully containing the destructive emotions I felt about leaving Mudi and about lusting for Audrey. When the record stopped my mind was gone. Joe came to talk to me, but he seemed to be on the other side of an aquarium wall. I couldn't hear him. I thought I might have an epileptic seizure; and this brought unspeakable fear. The spark of one wrong neuron would put me into apoplectic convulsions. Magic.

I knew full openness to all of life's forces was the challenge and excitement of taking drugs. "Go with the flow, neither accept nor deny," they said. But shouldn't one's concentration be absolute? If I couldn't control the energies around me, as Crowley said, then I would be "infallibly possessed by a demon." I gripped the edge of the sofa, and held my breath, determined to control my thoughts. From a corner I could hear something invisible rumbling louder and louder until it ran over me, and exited through the wall on the other side of the room. Every twenty seconds it ran over me like a locomotive. I was "possessed."

The continuous experience of that state would feasibly lead one to a padded cell in a straight jacket. Damnation would be the term applied to the extended form of the state, to be forever in fear and confusion, tortured by unseen forces.

"I'm possessed, Joe, I've been playing with magic; and now

I'm lost."

"What can we do?"

"Just hold onto me, I'm afraid if you let go I'll be swept away. Maybe someone knows what to do about possessions, and can help me, how about David Esterly?"

"I don't know," Joe said sympathetically.

Joe and Giles walked me from room to room, hoping to help; but everything frightened me — colors on a tie-dye sheet or the whistling of a kettle. I was especially afraid to be alone because the walls seemed energized with horrifying potentialities. For a while I lay on the floor in front of the fireplace, and grasped Joe or Giles whenever a surge of fear would overwhelm me. I reflected ironically that my prestigious past had brought me to a living room floor, totally devastated by the choices I had made. For the moment there seemed to be no solution to my dread fears except a return to the womb. And then the trip shifted directions as a loving light and glowing warmth descended over the room.

"Do you see it, Joe?"

"See what?"

"The room, it's glowing."

"No, what is it?'

"I think it's love. There's a force of love present."

The presence was bedazzling, and a glow of being radiated from every object. Where walls and furniture had seemed invested with sinister power before, they were now bedecked, bejeweled and humming with glorious, joyous, humorous love. Religious ecstasy momentarily turned me from Crowley's teachings to a God of love, a God of families and marriages. "Turn from your ways," I could almost hear Him say, "You are living in a generation where youth has chosen to go schizoid for entertainment. Will you join the insane, or will you help to build?" I turned to Joe.

"Doesn't love bind us all in the same trip?"

"Why, yes, that's right," Joe nodded.

"Giles, love is the answer for our lives."

"No, I don't think so."

How could he have missed such a blatantly obvious explanation? His coal black eyes stared into the fire. I grasped his hand, but it was hard and cold. "Love is the unifying principle?" I said hopefully.

"No, I think there are other explanations, power and selfishness, for instance."

"You're the devil, Giles," I said, as he picked up a blackened poker and turned a log, looking like Dr. Scratch himself, highlighted by the fire.

In the misty dawn I asked Joe for a book that would deal with divine revelations. *Paradise Lost* by Milton, he said, and as soon as bookshops were open I had an excellent copy.

There was, of course, a natural explanation for what had happened; but I was not then and am not now convinced that the merely natural explanation is sounder than the supernatural one. Several weeks later I heard the same locomotive sound in the Trinity Fellows Garden and realized that the roar and rumble of trucks on an arterial freeway produced it. Their frequent passing accounted for my being "run over" every twenty seconds. And the visions of glory could have been hallucinations. But three arguments militated against the natural explanation. First, the crux of my magical belief was that invisible forces shaped material reality. There was no reason why they couldn't have used trucks, teapots, or furniture. In addition, my experience had come dangerously close to that described in *Magick*; and so Crowley seemed somewhat realistic even if he was dangerous. Secondly, an indelible moral impression had been made about the rightness and wrongness of certain things; and this moral conviction had no discernible natural explanation. The love I had received from Joe and Giles was definitely good, while the alienation, loneliness, and schizoid separation were evil. And I went out the next day to buy *Paradise Lost*, a book about the Christian God of guilt and sin, confession and forgiveness, and Jesus Christ. Finally, the drug experience itself militated against the merely natural explanation. Nothing on drugs was merely natural. Instead all things were invested with deeper, resonating significance. I understood by my experience that I needed deeper, more cosmic answers, not simpler ones.

I didn't read *Paradise Lost* over the spring vacation but instead headed to Madrid once again to see Luis Arriola, a Spanish writer I had met the previous year and Lin, his Pennsylvania Dutch wife. Loyal to John Keats, I longed for "a beaker full of the warm South." And daily I read from Aleister Crowley's monumental *Confessions*. Luis knew immediately that I had come to Spain for pleasure. However it perplexed him to see that I was a broken man. The accumulated effects of promiscuity, drugs, and the occult had brought guilt and paranoia, an obsession with sex, and a terror of rejection, a general loss of self-confidence and low self-esteem.

Palm Sunday, 1970, Lin, Luis, and I tripped together on acid; and several days later drove to Salou, a beach resort on the East Coast of Spain. Luis said it was where Hemingway hung out in Spain. There Luis arranged an orgy but I couldn't participate. Instead I laughed at the studious pretense. For the next several days the three of us spent much of our time in Pepe's Bar on the beach, where we met Maria, a Czech barmaid.

Diary
Good Friday
March 27, 1970
More freak-out on life and animal forces. Pepe and his sidekick, *El Sordido Verdadero*, a cigar-smoking, sloe-eyed, creep have been keeping a noticeable distance from me. I'm freaked on Spanish Gothic Horror. Can't dig it. Took a couple of chicks to lunch, Maria-witch-like-happy-dumb broad. In ten minutes she said, 'I already know too much about you.' My eyes. It's a dog eat dog world. I come on like God only without warmth. I really know so little about finite human love. Luis appraises me keenly; but I feel the terror of his own soul. I hope I haven't freaked his friends.

Got gas on coming home that I was like a

puppy — part of Luis's attempt to get me moving. Just can't. I sometimes think I was born castrated — sex for everybody else. I can't be finite and still be idealistic.

Feel that I'm bringing the cold North with me to Lin and Luis. Don't want them to feel obligated, don't want to be a bother, want to be friend — all of me. More and more I stare into people's faces to see only horror, emptiness, greed. My toes are cold; and I've been cold so long. I want to come alive. And so, one year from Mudi's arms I am on the cold hillside.

I don't know why I was given life when I see so much hell around me. The psychedelic man has to solve the old problems of morality. Barren hillside. Where do I go from here? Middle class, upper class, heterosexual, homosexual, bisexual, head scene, the East, the West, friends and family, or the cold world, religious seclusion or the fleshy world. I was born to grow old and never know. I'm such a strange mixture. Now how do I make myself potent when I know that the energy I release can bring such hell? How I hate and love the person I am. How hard it is to show I care when I see such longing. My mind, body, spirit, soul yearn for the ecstatic explosion. I suppose the result of knowing paradise is dissatisfaction thereafter. Uh, oh, blah, gurch. I feel like a machine. How strange to be here and feel like a god, saint, demon — not a lover, not a man.

Luis composed a romantic poem for me — bemoaned my melancholy, chided my shadows, teased my spleen, rejected my remedies. He said he loved me; and I cherish that a lot. I admire his strength, energy, sanity and insanity. Food got us all sick tonight — what a ghost show. He's so tough to take this scene. He's Hemingway. I'm not. Twice to the Bay of Pigs, prize fighter, artist, lover, poet, scholar.

I wonder sometimes if I will have a breakdown and have to be sent home to Mommy. I wonder what happens to the little boys in so many men's souls. I think I'll go dig the sunrise. Wow, that Maria chick couldn't dig the sun — far out. Oh why?

Diary
Saturday March 28, 1970
Salou, Spain

I watched the sunrise from a lonely hill to the sounds of awakening birds, then bought presents for Lin and Luis, and walked through town alone and free, thinking of life as a wanderer. On Easter Sunday we left Salou. Maria's sad wild eyes told that she cared for me. In the long run I think I showed her that I actually loved her from afar and did not want the usual treatment she gives to customers and employers. I don't think I have ever seen eyes so rich with emotion, sensitivity and gypsy enchantment. She asked when I would return and why my answer was probably July. Her friend, Miri, also asked for my return and a postcard c/o Pepe's Bar, Salou, Spain.

April 2nd I said my good-byes to Lin and Luis as I boarded the train for Paris. I lightened the tedious train ride by concentrating on Crowley's *Confessions*. In Paris I called Mrs. Kantor who shyly mentioned that Veronique was living with her boyfriend, Paul. Veronique answered my call in a full, rich, languorous voice. I found her still spry, alert, mercurial. Paul, an actor, also displayed a quick, independent intellect. Fine and strong with fresh boyish narcissism, he was humble yet forceful in the nicest way. We spent enchanted hours over breakfast and walking through the Algerian section of Paris. I called poor Irene. Veronique had said she was suffering, but I found her divine — giggling from tears, laughing and crying at the same time, so happy to be happy that it evoked sadness. Leaving the open-air wonder of Paris, I boarded the bus for Beauvais and the airport.

At home in Cambridge, I found two American hippie friends, Karen and Alan, introduced to me by Mr. Clinton's brilliant son Billy. There was also a letter from Tom.

> Letter from Tom Ireland
> March 28, 1970
> Palo Alto, California

Dear Eric,

Thanks to you, I've been reading Captain Cook's journals because I enjoy the euphemisms of a man who really didn't know where he was on the face of the earth. I take lessons from the books that might not be intended: Cook writes of his second voyage, "it is practicable to go on discovering, even in the very depth of winter."

I want to do some global beach-combing. Let me know if you are interested. Mexico, Central and South America, East Indies, Australia, or anywhere. I've been doing survival training, sick of shellfish, would like to go where there's fruit on the trees and tropical disease. Been running around naked a lot lately, shores and forests, also falling down on the ground involuntarily, which as my friend from Arkansas says, ought to happen to a man if he is properly stoned.

Every time I get to feeling too light-hearted, I look at that picture of A. Crowley sucking his meerschaum and I feel bloodless and wicked again.

Tom

Diary
April 6, 1970

Alan did Tarot for me last night and tonight, surprising success, though I viewed the success at a distance as if half defending myself from submitting my intellect to this brand of analysis, and half finding myself almost routinely accepting the power of the Tarot. On the first try I asked what the possibilities for love for me were in the future. Got reply that signified love-power conflict, surprise hope in the future, strong outside forces and Devil as last card — love of natural exultation. I keep asking for magical evidence, clues to lead me into the practice. Cards implied conflict, fear of death.

Do I notice a hint of aggression in Giles? Does he fear me? His Tarot has been riddled with despair, evil, indecision, force, violence, and aggression. His face showed resignation to this reading. Where does the evil come from? Here I am hoping to love people. Hope.

Diary
April 27, 1970

On way down King Street was suddenly stabbed by really immobilizing back pain. Think I've pulled a muscle, but it never felt this bad. Wonder whether keeping Crowley's *Book of the Law* has anything to do with it. Indra at Bowes and Bowes said he had stabbing back pain for the week he carried the *Liber Legis*. Hate to destroy it — cost me 5 pounds.

I had groaned under the agony of that gray winter, but spring sun brought flowers, singing birds, and things better done than said. In May I met Anne, a wise Swiss girl who had read *The*

Odyssey in the original. She accompanied me to the 1971 May Ball. I was followed by the police in May, and almost arrested for possession of drugs, and for writing an article on Crowley in a pornographic newspaper.

The wild god Pan led our psychedelic troupe in the frolic of spring. Magic, exams, police, drugs — we danced to the heady music of a bacchanalia.

Giles prepared T-shirts for our group inscribed with obscene pictures and jokes largely derived from R. Crumb *Comix*. We proceeded to the Clare College Fellows Garden to harass a cocktail party with our anarchy. At the Clare garden I beheld a young lady gazing at me with large, sympathetic blue eyes.

"What's your philosophy?" she asked upon seeing the T-shirts.

"I'm a magician," I answered.

"How will you apply your philosophy?"

"Oh, I think I'll just study magic." I was a little stung by her firmness.

Her escort approached us, and stiffly appraised me. "These Americans just come here for a playboy degree, then they go back to America and make a lot of money in some big corporation."

"How do you plan to live on your ideas?" the beautiful lady asked.

"I don't know, how should I know, do you know?"

"Yes, I know."

"Good for you, you're so strong and you've got it so together."

"Come on, let's get out of here," her friend said, "look at that fancy little wiggle he's doing."

Diary
May 20, 1970

On Wednesday, May 14, I watched John and Rosemary get married. Lovely, but the thought of marriage seems so far away for me. Everything does. Identity problems, intellectual, emotional, sexual frustration. Where does all this misplaced energy come from? Why ask why?

Last week I received a startling letter from Pat, whom I met in Matala, Crete. Said she saw my face flash before her. I was trying to say by the look in my eyes that we did communicate. She also thought I was interested in a magical transformation, perhaps with another. I both wanted and didn't want to transform. How right she was! It is painful being born. My neurosis has perhaps peaked and I am coming down.

In my sorrowful state I feel depressed, worthless, ugly, stupid, unlovable and unloved, martyred, undirected, dilettante. My brain also aches with the thought of lost loves. How I wonder where I will go, or even if I should go. Will conventionality be the answer? Dribble, dribble. The worst film I could have seen was *The Pawnbroker* — searing fits of traumatic recollections.

Diary
May 24, 1970

I don't know why, but I think I broke a sacrament when I left Mudi; and now nothing remains but the obscene putrefaction of my own mind. Like Venus and copper, I am manifestly attractive and internally corrupt. Bull! The Tarot just told me this. Giles and Joe come down hard on my slow wit, incoherent mumbling and misinformed opinions. I feel weak, helpless and wishy-washy. No will, no fight. I whimper alone. Anne has been wonderful. She loves me so much and I am happy to know and be with her, but still I dream of Mudi.

I crammed for eighteen hours of exams with McKinnon, and received a median grade on the Economics Tripos. My Cambridge career formally ended a day after the May Ball with a telegram from Mr. Gardiner:

DEAR SIGGY:

IAN AND JOSIE GETTING MARRIED. WE WANT YOU IN THE WEDDING. COME. ALL EXPENSES ON US.

Theodore Dreiser wrote, "as I see him, the unutterably infinitesimal individual weaves among the mysteries a floss-like and wholly meaningless course — if course it be. In short, I catch no meaning from all I have seen, and pass quite as I came, confused and dismayed."

I had been blessed by a particular insight, if you could call it blessing, that Dreiser missed. I had seen berserk terror and stark, raving madness. If confusion and dismay were the simple sum of it, I might have stopped my search. The occult had taught me what psychologists imply, that there are vast, deep, and often terrifying forces behind our behavior. Terror had saved me from a Cretan exile, terror eventually led me to abandon drugs, and terror would lead me to meaning. I had followed the course of this world from academics to existential amorality, from existential amorality to occult oppression. I was more than dismayed; I was running scared, chased by my own shadow called damnation. My most hideous fear, however, would be my greatest blessing; for without that fear I never would have moved.

IV) STANFORD UNIVERSITY

CHAPTER 9: THE MOVE

I remember my affliction and my wandering
  The bitterness and the gall.
I well remember them,
  And my soul is downcast within me.
Yet this I call to mind
  And therefore I have hope:
Because of the Lord's great love we are not consumed,
  For his compassions never fail.
                        – Lamentations 3:19-22

Life seemed bearable in the frolic of Ian's wedding. The Gardiner's accepted my long hair and counter-culture arguments and it was good to see the old gang from Harvard. When I returned home to New York, however, I sank back into grief. I had begun smoking cigarettes and was feeling the bitter mouth, constricted chest, and excited brain from smoking. I stayed at home, read morbid epics like *Conan the Conqueror* by Robert Howard, and listened to AM radio. My mother's face did not hold the answers I needed for my troubled heart. She would say, "It'll be all right, O.K., O.K."

Now this picture formed in my mind: at the end of so much early promise lay only intellectual frustration, moral degradation, drugged confusion, and occult oppression. One whim, however, remained as a portent for good times: California, where people were exploring different lifestyles and where, at least, there was good weather.

I headed for California in August 1970 with a group of

Harvard rowing mates. I read John Fowles' *Magus* on the trip west. In California I would stay with Cleve Livingston, my crewmate from Harvard until I found a residence. Cleve had rowed for three Varsities and for two U.S. Teams at the Olympics. His sunny temperament, combined with California's cloudless skies, promised a respite from English cold and New York confusion.

Within a week of our arrival in California, a group of friends had gathered at the Livingston's for a hike into the Sierras of Inyo National Forest. Among others, our group included Cleve and his brother Mike, also an Olympic oarsman; Andy Larkin, the strong six-man from our boat; Tom Ireland, who was teaching at Stanford; Tom Tiffany and Paul Hoffman, two coxswains; Dan Nadaner, Tiffany's roommate at Harvard, and the other members of Dr. Livingston's family.

The Sierras are a particularly friendly range of mountains for climbers since there are few insects, an abundant water supply, and a mild climate. We started our hike in a flat, dry meadow that was surrounded by tall lodge poll pines and climbed into steep, cool forests. After about an hour of hiking at low altitude, we began a sharp ascent on brown granite. A crystal clear torrent of water dropped from a sharp ridge, and joyfully leapt down the mountain. In higher country we came to lush meadows and a flat stream. Over distant trees we could see minarets of granite, patched with snow, shining in the sun. At the end of the day we came to rest at the foot of these minarets. A hundred feet below our camp lay a tear-shaped lake; and towering above us rose a semi-circular range of granite peaks. As my eye followed the ragged edge of the distant peaks I saw thrones, altars, pulpits, spires and temples — high holy places of the Almighty.

For a week we played in the high country, exploring the rocky peaks, sliding on glaciers, swimming in streams, running through meadows. In the evening we traded stories and observed Cygnus the Swanfly through the Milky Way. Tom Tiffany suggested we develop a kind of evening ritual to honor the sacredness of the mountains.

After descending from the mountains, I vacationed with the Livingston's in Carmel-by-the-Sea where I began reading an occult book that had greatly influenced Crowley's magical path, and I began to write a screenplay based on the Conan novels. After Carmel, we returned to the Livingstons' home in Sacramento. The Livingstons encouraged my writing, but it was a hopeless task to write my screenplay. Conan's barbaric manners, his loincloth and sword, had long since paled as answers for life. It was a stroke of cruel irony that I, the defeated and depressed, should be writing a story about a strong-willed warrior. While I was muddling through Conan's battles, Cleve received a call from Bernie Thurber, co-captain of the Stanford crew. He needed a coach for the Stanford freshman crew on a volunteer basis. Cleve said he would be busy with law school, and so passed the phone to me. I said I could do it; but would they help me find some paying employment in the area? Bernie agreed to try.

The beginning of October I moved south, intending to move into Tom Ireland's old quarters in East Palo Alto, the ghetto. When I arrived, I found the inhabitants abandoning it like Oakies of the Depression with all their belongings packed on roofs of cars. The night before a few men had riddled the house with bullets; and now all the residents were leaving in fear. If the veteran hippies could not take the scene, I stood no better chance as a newcomer. And so I moved into the attic of the Stanford boathouse in Redwood City. The accommodations were humble, but satis-factory. There was a bunk bed, a desk, a filing cabinet, and rowing equipment in a small room. I had only a four-by-five rug as walking space. But the door opened onto a charming boat yard and the rolling green hills of Woodside in the West. I could look for work in the mornings, coach in the afternoons and go to Stanford in the evenings. Although genuinely fearful of the real world, and somewhat chagrinned at the meager Stanford facilities — after all I had rowed with Harvard and lived in great luxury — rowing was yet a contact with a world I knew and loved.

When Odysseus reached the limit of geographical lostness on

the island of the sea nymph Calypso, he did one thing he knew very well, he built a boat. Rowing could be a path back to wholeness, provided I coached faithfully and well. By early October, thirty-five freshmen were learning the elementary principles of conditioning and technique. I had also joined a New Age group at Stanford, called Servants of Awareness, devoted to the improvement of life through meditation and ritual. And, after an initial failure in love, that area seemed to be improving.

Diary
October 6, 1970

Shot down. Last Saturday I went picnicking up in La Honda with Joan, whom I met in the Stanford Coffee Shop. She is a Marilyn Monroe tragic figure. Her family background is Pasadena, father insurance salesman. She is blonde, beautiful like Candice Bergen, and wild-eyed from so many weird trips. In the past four years she has been to Berkeley, Detroit, Pasadena and now Stanford for college. I dug her wildness, her wisdom, and her hurt. I was there again, I wanted to help her out, wanted to love her, praise her — but, oh, the pain again. Will I love her forever? What does she need and want? Heavy. She keyed in on me and read my trip. Oh, God, Please, help me from the misery of my own selfish indecision.

Joan saw that I am wild, desperate, repressed. She also felt the weight of my oppressive consciousness and could not bear the strain. She told me tonight that a romance is now budding between her and a twenty-year-old in her dormitory. "A human relationship — you are a god on Olympus," she told me.

"Yes," I accepted the backhanded compliment, but it's so cold on the mountaintop.

I sit and wonder whether I have any choice

any longer. And why did Joan leave me? Confusion on my part, wishy-washy rap? Why do I feel so intently that I have nothing when the whole world tells me the opposite?

I've joined a *Cosmic Awareness* group and received good vibes from a girl in session but I shied away.

I'm happy that I have Cleve here. He's such a refreshing relief from my own consciousness. I love him. I love Tommy; I love his friends Spear and Jinny.

The Tarot was good to me. It concluded that I was the two of cups (love and will) and would strive to conquest. But sex is such a bad trip for me for this reason: I can't be cruel; sex is impossible without a relationship: but then I cheat. I leave. I'm fighting but my voice still rises from my lower abdomen like a distant foghorn, cold, unclear, suggestive but not explicit – haunting.

Diary
October 27, 1970

Last night I moved in with Diane. I have made the leap of faith that I figure is necessary to find love. She is soft, long, willowy; but the attraction is not entirely physical. In fact, it is more spiritual. I sense her warmth, her steadiness, and her equanimity. Spiritually, I feel she is wiser than I; for she understands that she loves me and that I must love her for it to work. She responds to my attentions and warmth, but requires that I lead the trip. She will not carry my weight. I am afraid.

Diary
November 3, 1970

In the way of magical progress I mention that I have joined a group called *Servants of Awareness*.

We meet twice a month at full moon and new moon to meditate and ritualize the admission of the higher cosmic consciousness into our lives. In this sense, we become channels for the universal mind that is usually blocked to us and to most humans.

I have found that the sessions are extremely enjoyable. The very act of joining a group of people who are religiously oriented is uplifting. Thus far I have been to three classes and two plans, or rituals. In the classes we discuss the literature: *Tibetan Book of the Dead,* and *Egyptian Book of the Dead, Revelation* from the Bible, *et al.* The plans have so far involved a fast from noon until the evening sessions; we wear no wool, leather or jewelry into the rituals. We start by meditating for half an hour, then enter the plan room which is usually set up with chairs in a circle. The plan is read by one of the servants who have tape-recorded it. The voice is solemn, comforting, even hypnotizing. We open the plan by a recitation of the Law of Love.

On October 10, we did a 'time-dilation' exercise, imagining ourselves in the past at distances of six months, one year, five years, and ten years.

Six Months Ago: Cambridge, England. The cold grayness. The suffocation of guilt and suspicious people. Snow on the commons even on April 8. Anne looks pale, haggard, and woebegone. Why have I not done more for her? One more cramped, cold, bad trip.

One Year Ago: Mudi writes a letter to say that it has been one year since we met and now it's over. Why?

Five Years Ago: Linda Muller, purple rugs, red bedspreads, Vicki and hung-up.

Ten Years Ago: freshman high school classes,
books, football. Greek history and the Parthenon.
Overall: Mudi, weight, and a bursting heart.
Can I ever love again? The room is heavy and one
girl looks grimly despondent.

After the prescribed studies, meditations, and rituals we anticipated being possessed by an entity from a higher plane. In fact, it was said, all our sessions had been transmitted through the founders of our group in trance sessions. And our leader, Ran, seemed able to deliver extraordinary information while in a trance. For instance, I asked for a trance reading on the age of an Egyptian talisman and for a purpose in life. My mummy's finger, I learned, was from 3400 BC; and I was told that I had joined awareness to realize myself and that beauty and blossoming would follow.

The marks I have grown to associate with occultism surfaced in our group. First, we hungered for a supernatural breakthrough: perhaps one night our ritual chanting would actually bring down the higher consciousness, and we would be transformed into new beings. A second quality that seems universal in the occult is the emotional addiction to small doses of truth that actually sustains one. We received personal encouragement and negative warnings from the rituals and trances, and for these we were greatly appreciative, yet we had not touched the realms of fear that I had known in England. Our path, it seemed, was not the demonic frenzy but the gentle, hypnotic sleep.

I am cautious of labeling occult experiences or even describing them because I am thoroughly convinced that the occult experience is largely imaginary, contentless and false. It is hard to put your finger on what actually happens when really almost nothing does happen. The constant hedging of claims in occultism, the refusal to say exactly what purpose some superstition may serve, contribute to the infuriating ambiguity of all occult claims. It may not be *that* phony, but it *is* phony. I can well understand why the magicians of Ephesus burned their expensive books (Acts 19:19).

Diary
November 15, 1970

I wonder if there will ever be a control to the radical changes of mood I go through. One moment I feel giddy and self-satisfied, happy to love Diane; and in the next moment my soul is screaming.

Last night Diane reproached me for my wishy-washy feelings toward her. I feared the pit of despair — a repetition of so many other insurmountable barriers. I remembered trying to convince Peta of my sincere love at her BU residence. Only now I realize how real my love was for her. And I remembered the battles with Judy as she cried, "You don't love me, you hate me!" And Anne, "You have broken my heart." I fought the darkness and hatred and I am happy for it. The light is there and it grows stronger. I shall do all I can to open my heart to Diane, and hope that the future will be good.

From the land of dangerous Calypso, Odysseus sailed to the island of the enchanted Phiaikians then on to Ithaca where he took lodging with his old swineherd. He met his son, Telemachus, there and eventually entered his own house disguised as a beggar. By steps he reassumed his position as king and husband. California, the Stanford crew, Diane and Servants of Awareness were my steps back towards purpose and self-understanding. But my will was only half the story, if that much. Someone was pulling for me on the other end. It was as though I had shot a basket and the basket moved to catch the ball. An altogether different, outside force was working behind the scenes.

One raining evening in December I wrote Mrs. Gardiner that I was searching after the Truth. I saw that without Truth I had no excuse for doing or saying anything. I needed a basis for action in life and it had to be unambiguous, absolute and true. But then I discovered to my surprise that truth was pursuing me. I met a man who had seen God.

I picked up Fred Wood hitchhiking on Alameda and Wood-side roads. A mercurial little leprechaun hopped into my car and proceeded to unfold the *Rhyme of the Ancient Mariner* from real life experience.

Diary

December 4, 1970

"Where are you coming from?" I asked.

"San Carlos."

"Live at Stanford?"

"No, going to classes. Sold my car and now I'm trying to make it on foot."

"Yeah, I don't know whether I want to make more money or learn to live on less."

"Either way it's hard," he said, appearing to know.

"Yeah, true."

"I've lived though, for two weeks with nothing to eat but coconuts on a desert island."

"Far out. Huh, What?"

"I was washed ashore with nothing on my back."

"No way! Tell me. I'll take you anywhere you want to go if you tell me the story. O.K.?"

"Sure.

"Two years ago I was sick of life, hated my job, didn't like my wife anymore. And so I decided to sail anywhere I could get. I bought a twenty-seven foot sloop for $2,200.00, put on six months of brown rice and a few weeks of fresh vegetables. My wife helped me, she was in favor of it; and on June 28, 1968 I sailed off from San Francisco.

"On the way to Hawaii a typhoon tore my jib sail and broke my rudder. I rigged a sea anchor to sail across wind. There wasn't enough drag on the stern, and so I had to rig some system of drag and tiller. I sailed into Hawaii and spent eight months there repairing her.

"I sailed out from Hawaii and a few months later was in the South Seas. One day I spied an island on the horizon about five miles away from the top of the mainmast. I hadn't slept for the past few days, and so I figured I'd rig a steering device and get a few hours sleep while we drifted into shore. I took a few jibs toward land because the wind was blowing diagonally off shore. As I was pushing the boom over, the sail filled with wind and pushed the boom back against me. My foot caught on a hatch cover, and since the sail was on the boom there was nothing to hold onto. In a second I was pushed into the water. I made a dive for the boat, but missed it by six inches and watched to see it sail over the horizon. I pinched myself to be sure I wasn't dreaming.

"The sun gave me some indication of where the island was and I started swimming and resting, swimming and resting. The sun went down and I had to navigate by the stars but I was becoming exhausted. I was moving only a few inches at a time. Finally, I stopped. I could go no further. I could barely keep above water and I figured I had thirty seconds to live. This was it. But I wanted to live. I wanted to do something worthwhile. A year before I didn't care, I wanted to die but now I wanted to live. And so I tried the one last thing. I prayed. The prayer went: 'If it is your will, Lord, I would like to live a little longer.' And I began to swim again: a miracle.

"I swam freely; there was no fatigue. And soon I could see the puffy clouds that form over land. I was close. I swam through a tangle of stinging tentacles — tentacles stinging me everywhere. They were Portuguese man-of-war. The pain was intense. I tried to pull them off, but couldn't. I tried to dive down to get out of them but couldn't. Finally, I swam through them; and they left me. I swam on and then ran into them again. I knew if I didn't get out, they would kill me. Again I swam through them.

"And then I heard a huge booming of waves on the coral reef. I had no choice. I had to swim towards the booming. As I got closer, I noticed the booming was greater on the left than on the right. I swam right to avoid the crashing waves. Soon I heard the booming behind me, and I was past the reef.

"Then I heard a softer crashing in front of me, and I figured I was close to land. I made a dash on the surf, and rode waves toward the shore. I had to keep in the wave. If I rolled or fell out, I would be crashed around on the bottom. I rode another set of waves; and on the next I was on coral. I grabbed hold of the coral tightly to keep from being crashed and torn on it, and to keep from being swept away by the undertow. I had to hold on, but the undertow was dragging me off. Just as I was about to let go another wave came in and swept me on. Then I was on a coral shelf. On all fours I crawled in until I found sand. I stood up, shaky. And I had seen it done, and figured it was a good idea. I got down on the sand and kissed it really seriously. I found some bushes, and got about four hours sleep. In the morning I felt reborn. This was June 28, 1969 one year exactly from the day of departure.

"I spent a week just resting, and letting my feet heal from coral wounds. And I spent another week wandering the island until I found a settlement. It was Christmas Island, the largest atoll in the South Pacific."

His eyes gleamed. I was shaking. I wanted to hug him, and tell him he was my savior, my fellow traveler. He was my Christ. I loved him, blessed him, thanked him and asked him to come to Awareness meetings. He said he would.

I dropped him at the Psychodrama Workshop on Forest Avenue. I said I was worried that people would hurt him.

He said, "Hey, man, these people can't take what I have; but I can give it to them, too."

I was enlightened. He was higher than I. "Oh, thank you, thank you," I told him.

"Hey, man," he said, "thanks for the ride."

I left in bliss.

Diary
December 9, 1970

Last night Fred came to the trance session. I couldn't breathe next to him. The white light off his light blue shirt and jeans was so bright that it was hard for me to look at him. I couldn't talk because most things I had to say seemed irrelevant by comparison to his heartfelt opinions.

After the trance, Fred talked to the group. Again I was dumbfounded. I wanted to kiss his shoes, and with tears in my eyes shout hosanna. I was in bliss just listening to him, and feeling his vibes. I did have tears running down my face as he talked. How simply he put it. "Love, that's all. Just give and take." So simple. I have since read Jesus' Sermon on the Mount. Love is all — God provides the rest, as he does for the fish, birds, animals and plants. What a revolutionary concept! Awareness, like Christ, implies that all that is important is to work towards Awareness of God. The rest comes as a manifestation of love.

I began to read the Bible to Diane, but she was not very interested because of her Roman Catholic upbringing which she was trying to overcome and reject. In addition, she would have felt better if I had more genuine interest in her and less in my mystical investigations. Probably she was paying for most of the rent and food, too. I was grateful for her hospitality, but was feeling a bit shabby. Soon I moved out to resolve the doubts. I was not going to love her. I was going to pursue the mystical interests; and I was feeling more inclined to celibacy, though it was late for that. Breaking away from Diane was hurtful for her, but important for me because of what I would learn next about sin. I was happy to leave her apartment and move in with male friends. A day later I flew to New York for a Christmas vacation, planning to preach the discoveries I thought I had made through Awareness, Fred Wood, and Jesus Christ summed up in the phrase, "God is love".

CHAPTER 10: FINAL REST

I learned that it is better, a thousand-fold, for a proud man
to fall and be humbled, than to hold up his head in his pride
and fancied innocence. I learned that he that will be a hero,
will barely be a man. He will merely be a doer of his work.
– George MacDonald, Phantastes

I went back to New York at Christmas to show mother that I was alive and happy, and also to communicate to her and my friends the word of Awareness. "Love is all, God is all, God is Love." My mother was at first disappointed with my spiritual plans and progress; but I tried to show her that other ambitions had kept me unhappy for much of my life. Awareness offered a faith to withstand the temptations of ego, greed and guilt.

One night before Christmas I needed exercise; and after several procrastinations, I walked off down Central Park West. At Eighty-ninth Street, I entered Central Park, which was covered with snow, and I walked across quiet ball fields, happy to be in open surroundings, reminiscing about Central Park, the football games and fishing. Standing on the edge of Castle Lake, I remembered the day Daddy came to meet me and help me take home 17 fish in a coffee can. Then, having walked over to Cherry Hill, I sat on a rock overlooking Fifth Avenue and Seventy-ninth Street, and meditated. The noise overwhelmed me. Could I ever contend with New York, could I ever let it pass through me without feeling its hassling? I doubted it.

After sitting on the hilltop I came down to Fifth Avenue and walked up to Eighty-first Street where I saw a couple playing in what looked like an oversized shell of a telephone booth but was actually a kiosk in front of the Metropolitan Museum of Art. I walked by and the girl motioned to me, "Look in here, listen to the Delphic Oracle."

"O.K.," I said, and perused the innards, staring at the man, thinking I knew him.

"You're Eric Sigward," he said, "I spotted you through the beard — I'm Peter Muller, Linda's brother."

"Far out.'

"This is Tish," he said. He had been married and divorced and Tish was his friend.

"I loved Linda in the fifth and sixth grades, I still do, I guess. I don't think you ever stop loving people. Relationship is forever."

Peter agreed and Tish said, "That's really beautiful, why don't you call her."

Peter agreed and when they left he said, "Do call Linda."

It was not merely meeting Linda's brother and the sense of infinite connectedness of things which amazed me, but the realization that I would actually have to defend my life and philosophy before Linda. And a genuine description of my life must include a defense of truth, love and a God called Cosmic Awareness. If she had once provided an impetus for touchdown runs and academic honors, again she would inspire me to reach ideals of the spirit. Like converging drops of water on a windowpane, it seemed that God's will and mine were becoming one.

I walked home and called Linda. She was out, and the next day she called and said she would "grasp the bull by the . . ."

She didn't finish the sentence. She was the same: cutely nasal, demure, desolate and honest.

I went to see her the next night. She was beautiful — moist lipped and gray-eyed like Athena. She had just finished her M.A. in French Literature at Columbia with a thesis on a surrealist poet. Surprisingly untainted by the cosmopolitan spirit, the only suggestions of New York compulsiveness were her smoking and the tendency to see lives in terms of career and marriage pieces.

But those were so slight. I felt myself involuntarily loving her all over again.

I had learned a few cosmological concepts about numbers and energy conservation. For instance, if energy was conserved I supposed love or hate was also conserved, that there would be an exact retribution on oneself for deeds of good or evil.

In addition, based on my experience, I believed and proclaimed that God was love. Armed with these truths I encountered Linda once again believing that this time all I had to do to love her was reveal the truths of life that I had learned.

We spent a few evenings talking, and took a walk through Central Park in the snow, feeling like we had been there since Sixth grade and things were still imponderable. Linda handed me a note one-day just as she had in the sixth grade.

> Dear Eric,
>
> I've been meaning to tell you some things for several days — since I first saw you. But I can't get myself to open up and say what I want to say — in a way I guess you overwhelm me. I do feel awed in your presence. So I will write to you. Not so good as spoken words perhaps, though better than silence — and more permanent, more tangible than both these means of communication.
>
> I think you are one of the most beautiful people I have ever known. I feel good just being around you, just knowing I know you. You remind me of one of my favorite poems — "Somewhere I have never traveled, gladly beyond" by e. e cummings:
>
> > somewhere i have never traveled, gladly
> > beyond any experience, your eyes have their silence
> > in your most frail gesture are things which en-
> > close me, or which i cannot touch because
> > they are too near
> > your slightest look easily will enclose me

though i have closed myself as fingers,

you open always petal by petal myself as spring opens

(touching skillfully, mysteriously) her first rose.

And it goes on. It is so amazing to me to be seeing you again — I try to just accept it, but I keep wondering how come, why — you have come at a good time. For so long I have been unaccustomed to feeling, to being, to letting myself go in the letting go of all the things around me that I'd almost quite forgotten what it is like to be with someone else, to talk to someone else, to accept someone else. And then you came, saying, "Just take my love, accept it." You are really most wondrous.

love is the every only god

. . . love beginning means return

. . . so truly perfectly the skies

by merciful love whispered were,

completes its brightness with your eyes

any illimitable star.

You are a star I love.

I left New York three weeks after arriving with lingering ties among many people and returned to Palo Alto to meditate in the sun. Linda was always in my thoughts, but I occupied myself with coaching crew.

Letter from Linda Muller
January 3, 1970
New York, New York

Dear Eric,

Well, you're gone — one brief flash of lightning and then the darkness again. I want to thank you for all you've given me. No one ever has given me so much in such a short time. I feel very close to you, and that is good. I can't express to you the depth of my gratitude.

I can't get your words out of my head. But it is good because that way we can be together in consciousness, in awareness of each other. I kept thinking that your leaving New York really did change everything — you know — energy levels . . . a pin drops in NYC and the stars reverberate.

I am trying not to feel separate from you. Last night for a while I was so sad. I couldn't get myself to be happy when I knew you'd be gone so soon. But then I got it together. Everything's going to be O.K. Oak, Oak. Oak.

See you soon. Be happy

I send you all my love.

All my love.

now all the fingers of this tree (darling) have
hands, and all the hands have people; and
more each particular person is (my love)
alive than every world can understand

and now you are and i am and we're
a mystery which will never happen again,
a miracle which has never happened before –
and shining this our must come to then. . .

forever is to give
and on forever's very now we stand
nor a first rose explodes but shall increase
whole truthful infinite immediate us.

— e. e. cummings.

I thought I was making real advances in Cosmic Awareness. Moreover, our group was planning a Stanford Education Conference on the meaning of life, and in January we were flooded with people interested in participating. Alain Naudé, an associate of the Indian teacher, Krishnamurti, offered to speak. He would bring Ali Akbar Khan, the Indian instrumentalist who accompanied Ravi Shankar. Convinced that a cosmic intelligence was ruling our lives and that faith could move mountains, I invited Linda to come. She decided, however, to remain in New York. And so, she receded from my life for the last time.

In spite of Linda's reluctance to come, I was energetically pursuing the mysteries of cosmic awareness. I perceived reality as infinite, not only because of the size of the universe but also because of its infinitesimal parts. Every drop of water could be broken into infinitesimally small but distinct parts. I called God the "One who gave order to infinity." Now this seemed feasible to me: if my mind is part of God's infinite creation, then in some sense God and I were one. He indwelled me by fact of creation. That God should be made flesh was perfectly comprehensible. In some sense, it occurred continuously in every human being. There was, however, one factor in my scheme I couldn't account for: sin and guilt, but that part of my chronicle shall have its appointed time.

I saw, too, that exhaustion could be a blessing from God. When one finally gives up the quest for himself, and allows himself to be, he is saved. Spiritual rebirth comes from loss and defeat. It is as if a snake spent all of his time chasing his tail to see if it existed. When he is exhausted he realizes he must rest or get food. Then he finds his tail actually alive and functioning to propel him or help him digest. In defeat is his true victory. It is the same with human personalities: They function best when they have forgotten themselves.

By mid-February I had started taking a class in Kundalini yoga, and was doing cabalistic meditations — meditations on the significance of Hebrew numbers and letters. And at this time we had our education conference. During the conference Alain Naudé, the keynote speaker, put me through a harrowing week, forcing me to look at the egocentricity of my own actions. He believed, like the psychiatrists, that simply looking at a problem would bring understanding and healing. His technique, while honest, did not provide practical solutions. Beyond a doubt, he convinced me of the shabbiness, irresponsibility and selfishness of my life; but this psychoanalytic ventilation did not, in fact, bring healing. Instead, I was left with the ponderous awareness of my own dark devices and hence, of my despair. I had to conclude that despite awareness of certain cosmic mechanics I was still a fundamentally poor excuse for a human being.

The crew at this time was wearing Cosmic Awareness T-shirts with rainbows on the back; and we were working in splendid California weather. Unlike the frozen Charles, our estuary in Redwood City was usable all year long. Only the stiff spring winds that came up in afternoons measurably affected our workouts. Otherwise, Stanford has a superb course; and on spring mornings we watched the sun rise over the Milpitas Mountains and glow golden on the smooth surface of the water.

The eighteen men who remained by late February had been devoted to me and to the sport. Their sympathy and integrity had encouraged my coaching and I had grown to love them. However, I wanted to give them an answer for life that went beyond their fondness of rowing and I would not encourage them to make the mistake of imbalanced devotion to crew that I had made at Harvard.

Both our boats showed physical and technical ability. They had grasped the principles of a fast catch, hard pull-through, and clean release. Moreover, they were able to establish a swinging rhythm, and maintain power for long pieces. Our first boat stroke, Dick Kirby, a pre-med student from Seattle, proved to be mentally tough and cool under pressure.

Early that spring we faced the varsity in a practice row. As our boats drew together, I repeated the style and words I had learned from Harry.

"We're going to take a few two-minute pieces with the varsity," I said, "Take five to build it, then we'll row the body of the piece at thirty-two strokes per minute. Cox, take ratings. Keep your oars buried, quick catches, clean finishes. Concentrate in your own boat."

In a moment my freshman were off on their first test. I watched their zeal with pleasure — heads snapping as they grabbed a quick catch, muscles and sinews taut on the pull-through, faces torn into grimaces of strain, and the rhythmic settle. In ten strokes they were ahead by a deck, and they had open water by the finish.

I piloted my launch over to the exhausted freshmen, grinning broadly. "Well done, phenomenal." They were recovering with hilarious laughter, and we continued to beat the varsity soundly until they retreated to work on style. A satisfying racing season lay ahead, and we finished the year with a 9-2 record, and came in fifth in the West Coast Sprints.

Early February Fred Wood joined me at the boathouse, and helped drive the coach's launch during practices. Largely because of him I started reading my old King James Version — the Sermon on the Mount. Because of my commitment to cabalistic meditations and yoga, I had turned vegetarian; and I was supporting myself by means of government food stamps and a job at Bucko's Leather Shop in downtown Palo Alto.

On one of those crisp, clear afternoons that brings joy to the California Chamber of Commerce — perfectly warm, and smog-free–I bumped into Tom Ireland on the Stanford campus. He was talking to a short young man with bare feet, a light-brown cowlick, and a clean-shaved face. His name was Timothy English. Tom was no stranger to the mystic paths. He himself had been doing dawn meditations at a Zen temple. And so I was not surprised to find him talking with Timothy about spiritual matters. Timothy turned to me with an open Bible in his hand.

"It's all in here, man," he said, smiling broadly.

"What?" I said.

"Jesus."

"Oh, yeah, I know, Jesus was a cosmic philosopher; and

potentially we can all be like Jesus if we open our minds to the cosmic intelligence."

"No, man. Jesus is the only way to God. There is one mediator between God and man, the man Christ Jesus."

"Timothy, I've read the Sermon on the Mount, and even Jesus said, 'Don't swear: neither by heaven for it is God's throne; nor by the earth; for it is His footstool . . .'"

"'Nor by Jerusalem, for it is the city of the great King . . . ,'" Timothy finished my quotation.

"Why should I swear by Jesus if he himself said not to swear?"

Timothy did not answer my question but looked at me with bright blue eyes. "I perceive there is an opening here and where there is an opening one no longer needs to knock."

I sensed we were in a mystical sweet communion, and smiled knowingly; he smiled back.

I said, "I've been very interested in occultism for the last year or so. I'm convinced of spirit forces behind daily reality."

"Yes, I know," Timothy concurred, "my bed spontaneously combusted one night because I was practicing black magic."

"No kidding. That seems to be a problem with the occult," I said, "I think I was demon-possessed or close to it."

"I've been plagued by several demons — lust and pride, especially. Pride is the harder one to fight. I think I know a lot."

"You've been plagued by lust, too?"

"Yes, I was a sex pervert. I used to take little boys and girls to my room to seduce them."

"I think drugs can open your mind to almost any kind of behavior. I'm not at all surprised by Charles Manson's philosophy."

"My roommates used to call me a drug fiend."

"Was it acid?"

"No, heroin, I'd do anything to get a fix."

In short shrift Timothy confessed his deepest sins and proved his identification with me in vice. He was twenty-six, and had been raised an Orthodox Jew on a Kansas farm. At Stanford he turned to radical politics and the other activities of the counterculture. As he talked one characteristic distinguished Timothy from any person I had met. I would call it mercy. It poured from him like a river as he lectured, informed and corrected me.

"How did you turn to Christianity?" I asked.

"I was in Kansas for summer vacation; and my doctor asked if I ever gave thanks. 'Give thanks? I don't give thanks, I'm a radical.' He said I should give thanks to God, and told me to read a book called *Oaspe*. I forgot what he said, and returned to California. I was driving up in the hills one day and my car broke down. A truck pulled up and a man got out. He said, 'Open your hood.' I opened the hood and he waved his hand over the engine. Then the car started. He left and said, 'You haven't read *Oaspe* yet, read it.' I read Oaspe which is about cosmology, how God created the world, and that led me to Jesus."

Timothy talked with me for four hours that afternoon, perfectly at ease with my questions, but he was unable to convince me that Jesus was materially different from Cosmic Awareness. He left me with a warning, "Beware of Satan. Jesus called him a liar and a murderer. He'll give you ninety per cent of the truth, and then lie about Jesus. Peace be with you, brother."

After leaving Timothy, I went down to the Servants of Awareness room in the Nitery Building close to White Plaza. Our leader and trance medium, Ran, was filing papers.

"Ran, we accept the teachings of Jesus according to the channeling we've received, right?"

"Yes, that's right," he replied.

"Then, why is our group always concerned about money? Jesus said not to be anxious for what you eat or drink."

"Yes, but we have to raise funds."

"Jesus said to seek His kingdom and all else would be added unto you."

"You know something, Eric, you're a half-assed dude."

Ran was a spacey star-child type, and didn't rile easily; but when I pressured him on the exact words of Jesus he blew up. I filed that with Timothy's last comment about Satan, and lived the next two weeks as usual in vegetarianism, yoga, Cosmic Awareness, crew and leather work.

Wednesday, March 10, I chanced to meet Timothy again at the New Age Food Store in downtown Palo Alto. I was suffering from several days of hateful thoughts. Saturday I had gone through an uncomfortable argument with Jinny Sart, a girl with an evil greedy gleam in her eye. Sunday, Monday, and Tuesday I did cabala meditations, and had gotten unbearable headaches. Wednesday I had awakened glum, as usual, and stumbled disgruntled to work at the leather shop. At eleven or so I went to New Age to eat, and found Timothy.

"Hi Timothy."

"Brother Eric! I've been thinking about you."

"I'm not making it, Tim, do you have time to talk?"

"Sure, Eric. My Jewish mother sent me some spices from Kansas. Let's get salads, and eat in my camper."

While we were waiting for our salads, Timothy began reading a book on Buckminster Fuller; and I saw Ran enter the store.

"This is my friend, Timothy English, Ran; he's an architecture student at Stanford."

Ran looked at Timothy's book, "Buckminster Fuller is into geodesics," Ran opined.

"Geogonals," Timothy one-upped him. "He gave up geodesics two years ago."

Ran sat silently beside us waiting for his order, then left. Timothy and I carried our salads to the camper where Timothy prepared spices and oil. "You feel like a lamb among wolves, don't you?" he said.

"Yes, that's apt. How did you know?"

"Jesus said he would send us out like lambs among wolves."

"That's beautiful."

"Timothy, I think my problem has to do with sex. I just can't get it straight."

"That's because you're sinning."

The words flashed like a purifying fire. "Look, Eric, I'd love to have all kinds of sex but I know it's sin. God intends sex for marriage. It won't work any other way. You've sinned, Eric; but those sins were forgiven by Jesus at the cross."

The cross: for the first time in view of sin the cross became comprehensible. Before it had been meaningless but now I understood the *via dolorosa*, the blood and the agony of Jesus. His suffering healed me.

Timothy opened his Bible at Matthew 11:28 and read. "Come unto me, all ye that labour and are heavy laden, and I will give you rest. Take my yoke upon you, and learn of me; for I am meek and lowly in heart: and ye shall find rest unto your souls. For my yoke is easy, and my burden is light."

I began to weep as Timothy read, and then laugh.

"Praise the Lord!" Timothy said.

In what seemed like eternity forced into a second, I saw Jesus bleeding on the cross. I saw that I had traveled the world, largely by motorcycle, and was now being called by God himself to faith in his Son, Jesus Christ.

"Yes, the Lord, I'm being touched by God."

"Do you accept Jesus as your Lord and Savior?"

It was no longer a question: I could see and believe. "Yes, I do."

"You're a Christian now."

At 1:15 PM we went to Tom Ireland's creative writing class at Stanford. He had asked me to talk on magic and mysticism. I began my discussion predictably, gloomily stating that it was necessary to face one's true despair, that even the best actions were essentially egotistical; and then as an answer for life I announced that Jesus was my Lord.

Tom, whom I had known from the First Form at Horace Mann, darted slightly backwards on his chair that he was balancing on two legs. And his writing class began to interrogate me but what relief I felt for my soul to get that thought off my chest! Timothy had said I must confess the name of Jesus and see the demons flee. For the remainder of the class I sat silently while Timothy English answered the challengers for he readily understood that this infant Christian was not ready for the fray.

"What do I do now, Timothy?" I asked as we left the class.

"You need to do three things to increase your faith: Read the Bible, pray and talk to people every day. Peninsula Bible Church has meetings at the Geology Corner on Sundays. You might like to attend them."

Timothy hugged me, and departed in the joy of the Spirit. I have not seen him since.

> Diary
> Sunday, April 4, 1971
> Palm Sunday
> I went to Peninsula Bible Church classes in Bible study this morning. I was humble and timid around so many bright, loving people. I admired their faith and openness. I pray for them, dear Lord.
>
> This evening I broke the black spell of Awareness. Perhaps this marks the end of any sort of occult control in my life. I started hating Awareness for its results. The rituals have been filled with zombies and they have been getting grimmer and grimmer as time went on. I have been suspicious of trance readings on sex, marriage, homosexuality and religion. Tonight I saw Katie go so low I had to help her. In ritual she started to cry. I held her hand. David Brewster tapped me on the shoulder. I told him to get lost. The spell was breaking.
>
> Then Ran began to read this neo-Nazi doctrine of Awareness and the New Being. It was pathetic to see this weird creep trembling, insecure, pale, unhealthy, morbid, sick reading those assertions. I

blew up and told him and the class that the text was bull and that they could keep the New Being. The ministers look like such tools of darkness. I feel sure that Awareness is an occult force of the devil and the dark lord is whipping all the ministers. I threw off my robe and stalked out, saying 'Peace in the name of God and Jesus.'

Awareness had recently been a bummer for me. My head would hurt whenever I was near the class. Louis looks like a really good Dracula. The morality of the servants is abominable. The rituals are occult in that they force people into mind traps where you are always looking for an effect. Touch the sword, light the candle and see God. Bull. You have to live by God's Word through Jesus Christ. Peace.

Here ends my magical diary, really begun with my first drug trip in Crete August, 1969. And so, two years later I am a soldier of Christ with an awareness of the dangers of occultism. Now begins my Christian life. Hello, sweet Jesus. Happy Palm Sunday.

At our next crew meeting I thanked the gentlemen for their devotion to rowing and to me. Hoping to spare them some of the mistakes I had made, I noted that Jesus had unambiguously claimed to be the Truth; and I believed it.

"No professor has ever told me, 'This is true, you need this in order to live.'"

"My life," I said, "has found its final rest in Jesus Christ and I wish you would find Christ, too."

EPILOGUE 1975

'Are you thirsty?' said the Lion.
'I'm dying of thirst,' said Jill.
'Then drink,' said the Lion.
'May I — could I — would you mind going away while I do?'
The Lion answered this only by a look and a very low growl...
'I daren't come and drink,' said Jill.
'Then you will die of thirst,' said the Lion.
'Oh, dear!' said Jill, coming another step nearer. 'I suppose I
must go and look for another stream then.'
'There is no other stream,' said the Lion.
– C. S. Lewis, The Silver Chair

One Sunday, soon after my conversion, I went over to Seminar '70 at the Geology Corner. There I found two or three hundred Christian students. The leader of the group, an undergraduate, was filled with good humor. After a brief period of singing and sharing of personal problems, the large group broke up into ten smaller classes for study. I remained in the original room, and listened to Dave Roper, a pastor from Peninsula Bible Church, teach Bible Study Techniques.

"Let's outline the three principles of Bible study:

Observe. That means read a passage fifty times if you have to." Dave drawled in a slow Texas accent. "Then, interpret. That means try to find the message the Lord has for you in this passage. And, apply. See how the message fits into your life."

His slow, orderly style was easy to follow.

"Now let's cover some grammatical principles. How many

cases can a noun take? Let's use the Latin case system as a reference." As the class recited nominative, genitive, dative, accusative, ablative, I rejoiced because reason had returned to the world.

One afternoon, I introduced myself to Dave at the Stanford track. He invited me to lunch later that week; and on subsequent weeks we studied passages from First Peter with Brian Morgan, a Stanford senior. For the next three years Dave discipled me in the principles of Christian living, helping to rebuild the broken walls in my life with faith, love and truth.

Almost the first phrase I heard from Dave was "Jesus was a methodical man." A great deal can be gleaned about Dave and Jesus from this statement; but what it has meant to me is that in Christianity life is the issue; its tenor, pace, and quality — not doctrine or ideas only.

A year later I became an intern at Peninsula Bible Church and learned three important areas of truth. First, God's picture of the Church is an organism, a body. The Body of Christ functions to heal the many fractures we experience in this world. Secondly, we have, as Timothy said, a real spiritual enemy in Satan who intends to destroy our lives through deception. Only a faith in the person of Christ can defeat the wiles of this supernatural foe. Finally, our present relationship to God is described by the New Covenant between God and man. God has made a unilateral, unconditional commitment to man who obtains the favor of life by faith alone.

I was baptized April, 1971 according to Christ's commandment; and that summer I returned to New York to visit and explain a new change to friends. Of course, I met with skepticism; but I trust that time has erased faddist suspicions in my friends' minds.

In New York I reread *Screwtape Letters* and *Miracles* by C. S. Lewis and said "Oh my gosh, Christianity, *that's* what he's talking about." His erudition, wit and hard work on behalf of Christ continue to inspire my own walk of faith.

At the end of the summer, I received a call from John Crocker, my Harvard roommate who was in Boston.

"What's up?" John crackled.

"I'm a Christian, John."

"When are you returning to California?"

"Sunday."

"I'll be down Friday."

Big John was even more enormous than usual. His six-foot-six-inch frame was growing corpulent.

"What's this about Christianity, Eric?"

"I believe Jesus is the Son of God who died for our sins."

John's computer whirred briefly. "I accept that, what do I do?"

"You accept Jesus into your heart as Lord and Savior."

"OK, let's do it. Where do you want to pray? How about by your bed?"

In that instant John gave his life to Christ. His sister, Debby, followed his example a year later; both eventually migrated to Peninsula Bible Church in Palo Alto.

Lest anyone think that Christ is a quick panacea for human ills, I will record several incidents following our conversions. John, for instance, shared a flat with me in Mountain View, California. One night John came into my room and in frenzy said, "We have to pray, Satan's really attacking me, he's making me throw up." He'd been vomiting all night. We prayed, and he cooled down. Other times John would cry out during the night; and I would comfort him with a "Peace in the name of Jesus Christ." Conversion for him has meant instant salvation but it is taking years to develop the piety, purity and constancy that Christianity requires. Joyfully, God is doing a mighty work in John.

It has been difficult for me to accept that I actually have chasms of guilt and sin. I had thought that problems were merely conscious attitudes that would soon dissolve as I grew in faith. Instead I am staggered to realize how dreadfully deep these wounds are, extending back to the Garden of Eden. I continue to give thanks, however, that in Christ there is actually hope for the human condition.

How, then, does my American dream find a place in historic Christianity? It does not in the role of any useful addition to Christian faith. It must be realized that biblical faith never needed culture for its expansion. On the contrary, Christianity broke the paths for civilization; seizing all levels of peoples and lifting all alike to its own heights. The American culture is only one more field that must be plowed and planted by Christian faith.

EPILOGUE 2003

As soon as God had carried us safely to New England, and we had builded our houses, provided necessaries for our own livelihood, reared convenient places for God's worship, and settled the civil government, one of the next things we longed for and looked after was, to advance learning and to perpetuate it to posterity, dreading to leave an illiterate ministry to the churches, when our present ministers shall lie in the dust.
— New England's First Fruits

Thirty-two years have passed since my conversion. A full account of events from then until now would occupy at least one volume. And another work that is almost completed discusses theology, a logical sequel to this personal memoir. When I converted, I was Stanford freshman crew coach. I thought I had had enough of the barbarically physical life. I had been good in some academic subjects, and wanted to pursue academics into the Christian realm. After all, even Conan could dance the complex steps of the Cimmerian gavotte. Therefore, I occupied myself with biblical and theological studies. There were those who helped me and others whom I helped. There was always someone above and someone below.

The early part of the 1970's continued to be Stanford university years, since I lived in or around Palo Alto and studied or taught the Bible on campus. Academic years Dave Roper took me under wing, and I joined the ministerial institute at church where he was a pastor. There at PBC I studied Bible and theology.

Refugees from the hippie cataclysm marked the church. Many of the young members were the fallout of the 60's. They were the burned-out, ex-druggie misfits. Some of the girls were unwed mothers and I shared a house with three of them. Some were emotionally scarred. One, I remember, had lived in doorways in San Francisco after quitting Ken Kesey's Merry Pranksters. She was poetic, sad, and loopy. Another was a most beautiful blonde California girl, guilt-ridden by her abortion. God had called the weary and heavy-laden into this church.

Pastor Ray C. Stedman's amusing sermon delivery flavored the ministry. Affectionate disciples copied his style and there were Ray clones everywhere. You pat your belly with the left hand, at the same time move your Bible up and down in your right hand, now smile and shake your head as though saying "no." Squint your eyes. Ray was developing his own "New Covenant Ministry" derived from 2 Corinthians 2-6. He emphasized the passivity of the Christian to the Holy Spirit's ministry within him. It was a laid-back message in tune with Ray's mellow personality.

In retrospect, it does not seem thoroughly Reformed, because it had elements of perfectionism and Arminianism. It had no real place for the majesty of God's law or the abiding nature of sin, but he tried to teach the activity of the Holy Spirit and the passivity of man in redemption and discipleship. In these teachings, he was wise and well-meaning.

Summers, I studied Greek and Hebrew at Western Seminary in Portland, Oregon. During the academic year, I ministered on or near the Stanford Campus, as Dave did — witnessing to Christ's redemption, praying for the campus, and conducting small Bible studies. I would meet a student or professional who wanted to study and pray and often the relationship lasted several years. I would teach Bible studies in private homes or on campus. Sundays, I used to teach courses for the campus student fellowship. For instance, I taught the works of C. S. Lewis to Stanford Christians.

Summer 1974 I moved to Portland, and became a student at

Western Seminary. Life and work kept me out-of-doors in the perpetual rains of the Pacific Northwest. Another fact of nature gradually dawned on me. Constant rains can be benevolent, warm and gentle. Pleasure from the weather is a great secret of the Pacific Northwest. My eyes lifted up and around. The most immense trees and rivers the world has ever seen surrounded me. Roses bloomed everywhere. Oxygen permeated the air.

Spring 1975 I worked for Inter-Varsity Christian Fellowship at Reed College. David Stiles, a fellow student at Western, urged me to read Reformed theologians and transfer to Westminster Theological Seminary in Philadelphia. September I transferred, became Reformed, joined the Orthodox Presbyterian Church and earned the Master of Divinity and Master of Theology Degrees. From 1978-1983 I performed missionary and pastoral labors as a licensed preacher in the denomination.

I served in 1980 as full-time pulpit supply for Grace Orthodox Presbyterian Church, Lynchburg, Virginia. I returned in 1981 to New York City where I held odd jobs and continued to preach. I landed my first decent job in 1983 as office manager for a garment buying office owned by a Horace Mann classmate, John Cohn. From 1987-1989 I traded stocks as a stockbroker, and found the world of mammon to be witty, intelligent and fun.

The 1990's were my computer-hacking decade. I did accounts receivable, controller work, and garment label manufacturing for my own company on PC's. From 1992-1996 I edited and published *The Works of Cornelius Van Til, 1895-1987 CD-ROM.*

If Joseph Conrad's *The Heart of Darkness* was "a little too dark," then the reverse was true of theology. The heart of light is much too bright. At Westminster I learned a new teaching of the relation between God and man's free will. God must save me by his Spirit prior to the act of faith. As a sinner, I am dead in sin and have no free will to choose God. I am by nature in bondage to sin, unwilling and unable to come to God by faith. God's Spirit must intervene. I became Reformed.[3]

I came to believe that God elected, called, regenerated and justified me freely by his grace and in his good time. The small distinction regarding the relation between divine sovereignty and human free will proved to be a philosophical Copernican revolution. First, it made the glory of God the center of all knowledge. It opened up church history, for it showed the same debate between Augustine and Pelagius in the fifth century, and between Luther and Erasmus in the sixteenth, and between the Reformed and Arminians at the Synod of Dordt in the seventeenth. Divine sovereignty opened up the world of knowledge. Whereas the fields of knowledge like politics, business, science and the arts had seemed irrational; they now seemed like mountains of reason. I no longer followed the Arminian free-will gospel of C. S. Lewis or Ray Stedman. I began to conform to the historic, Reformed creed, *The Westminster Confession of Faith.*

The question of free will was the departure point for me. Whence, I also departed from the antinomian dispensationalism in favor of covenant theology. I departed from being an adult-baptizer to being a paedo-baptist. I gave up perfectionism in favor of the majesty of God's law and the continuation of sin. I gave up evidentialism in apologetics in favor of presuppositionalism, for I saw that all arguments are based on *a priori* assumptions. I abandoned belief in the continuation of charismatic gifts, to belief that final authority is in Scripture. I became a Puritan with reference to Sunday Sabbath observance. I became an amillennialist instead of a dispensational premillennialist.

There were times at Westminster I just sat on the edge of my bed and wondered what I was doing there. I was making a doctrinal odyssey from Sicily to Scotland. That is to say, I was on the road of a long, slow life-change. Sermon preparation took twenty hours for each; and I have preached about 300 sermons in the last 20 years. I made new friends and practices. It all occurred silently and without geography. The journey took place through books; and it was to be intensely private and personal.

ENDNOTES

1. When I first wrote this, I thought Lewis was cogent. I have changed that view since learning the Reformed faith. I believe Lewis is mistaken here in speaking about the naturalist and the supernaturalist. He should have contrasted unbelief, whether naturalistic or supernaturalistic, with Christian faith. That might have helped clarify the issues.

2. By 2002 ergometers have become so much a part of training that there are collegiate, national and international ergometer racing championships where numeric results call the winner. The first ergometer of 1966, described here — with a flywheel like a millstone and an oar handle attached to a ratchet gear — has been replaced by a svelte, hi-tech device with an air-resistance wheel and an electronic counter. Ergometers now fill the second floor gymnasium space of Newell Boathouse.

3. Van Til, in his *Defense of the Faith*: "If God was to be maintained in his incommunicable attributes the Spirit of God, not man, had to effect the salvation of man. The only alternative to this would be that man could at some point take the initiative in the matter of his own salvation. This would imply that the salvation wrought by Christ could be frustrated by man. Suppose that none should accept the salvation offered to them. In that case the whole of Christ's work would be in vain and the eternal God would be set at nought by temporal man. Even if we say that in the case of any one individual sinner the question of salvation is in the last analysis dependent upon man rather than upon God, that is if we say that man can of himself accept or reject the gospel as he pleases, we have made the eternal God dependent upon man. We have then, in effect, denied the incommunicable attributes of God. If we refuse to mix the eternal and the temporal at the point of creation and at the point of the incarnation we must also refuse to mix them at the point of salvation." *The Works of Cornelius Van Til, 1895-1987 CD-ROM* (Jackson Heights: Labels Army Co., 1997).

INDEX OF NAMES

Italy, 18, 29, 68-69, 72, 121, 123;
Isle of Capri: 71-72; Rome:
16, 62, 67-72, 77, 103, 117,
121, 123

Kanon, Joe, 28, 111, 121,
123-126, 128, 136-138, 145
Kantor, Veronique, 71, 121,
141-142
Keats, John, 28, 54, 108, 116, 139
Kesey, Ken, 115, 126, 182
Khan, Ali Akbar, 168
King Crimson, 136
King, Martin Luther & Coretta
Scott, 62
Kirby, Dick, 169
Knight, III, John S., photos,
113
Krishnamurti, 168
Kundalini Yoga, 168

Larkin, Andy, 49, photos, 150
Lebanon, Beirut: 61, 68, 76, 103
Lewis, C. S., 32-33, 39, 177-178,
182, 184, 185 n. 1
Lindon, Irene, 71, 121, 142
Livingston, Cleve, 48, photos,
150-151, 153
Livingston, Mike, 150
Luther, Martin, 184

MacDonald, George, 163
Magick, 134-135, 138; See also
Crowley, Aleister
Magus, The, 150
Mander, Nick, 135
Manson, Charles, 127, 171
Maugham, Somerset, 133
May Ball, photos, 116-120, 143,
146

McKinnon, John, 78-80,
photos, 105-106, 110, 112-
113, 119, 139, 144
McKinnon, Rosemary Fletcher,
115, 144
Merry Pranksters, 115, 182
Metcalf, Walter, 17
Mexico City Olympics, 37, 49-
51, 74
Miller, Coach "Moose," 22
Miller, Myron, 22
Morocco, 104, 110, 112-113,
132; Marrakesh: photos,
110-111, 113, 118, 121;
Tangiers: 112-113
Muller, Linda, 14-15, 23, 28,
53-55, photos, 154, 164-166,
168
Muller, Peter, 164
Munch, Edvaard, 106
Murphy, Shawn, 54-55
Musson, Giles, 135-138, 143-
145
National Merit Scholarship, 13
Naude, Alain, 168
New Age Food Store, 173
New England's First Fruits,
181
New Testament, Matthew:
174; Sermon on the Mount:
160, 171; Luke: 173; Acts:
155; 2 Corinthians: 181; 1
Peter: 182; Revelation of
John: 135, 154
New York, 13, 16, 19, 29, 33,
36, 47, 55, 62, 73, 75, photos,
107, 117, 149-150, 161, 163,
166-168, 178
Newell Boathouse, 27
Norway, 106

INDEX OF SUBJECTS

ABOUT THE PERSONS

Clint Allen: the stroke of the undefeated 1966 Harvard heavyweight crew. He immensely enlarged the photo displayed here so that he was able to use it for his office wallpaper. He was a flamboyant athlete who liked "old whiskey, young women, fast cars, and lots of money." He became a founding investor in Blockbuster Video. Only Clint and I did not make the Harvard Athletic Hall of Fame from our "Golden Era of Harvard rowing." Perhaps we were too small. He resides in Cambridge, Massachusetts with his family.

Johanna Andersen: Mudi's best friend came from Copenhagen to Cambridge, and studied English. She was John McKinnon's girlfriend until he met Rosemary whom he married.

Luis and Lin Arriola: A passionate lover of Spain, Luis was a Cuban living in Madrid with his wife Lin when I met him. He was a boxer, writer, professor of English, and had fought in the Bay of Pigs. He managed prizefighters, and admired Hemingway. He knew Fidel Castro personally, and did not like him. He and Lin showed me an unusual type of hospitality in Spain the spring of 1970. With a potpourri of sins on the table, to say the least, this was not your average junior year abroad. Lin was his Pennsylvania Dutch wife.

Nick Bancroft rowed for the Harvard heavyweight crew in the early '60's. He is a descendant of several generations of Harvard oarsmen. Nick supports the crew program as a Friend of Harvard Rowing.

David Braga supported me in my bid for the Porcellian Club by wining and dining me in Cambridge bistros. He served in Vista and the U.S. Marines in the Vietnam era. He has a daughter at Georgetown and a son at Harvard. He manages businesses in New York.

Judy Bruce: We met in Social Relations 120, Harvard's interpersonal psychology course. We spent time together in Rome before I entered Cambridge University and she began a year of study and travel in the Middle East. She works for the U.N. Population Council. She has two daughters; one is a movie starlet. She became a world-renowned advocate for female rights.

Charles, Prince of Wales: The press avidly followed his life and found him far more exciting and stimulating than his Cambridge studies would have predicted. At Cambridge he seemed to follow the course of any average Joe.

Billy Clinton, the son of Mr. Clinton, is a fast friend and guru. Archetypal hipster, he almost earned the Ph.D. from Columbia University in clinical psychology. Recently, he spent time in Russia and plans to return. He has one son at Amherst College.

William R. Clinton: My senior history teacher at Horace Mann, taught and was Dean of the school 1953-1997. He resides in Riverdale, NY.

Conan the Barbarian emerged as a huge success — first during the Depression in pulp fiction, then in comics and finally in the movies with Arnold Schwarzenegger playing the Cimmerian in his first role. Robert Howard's hometown of Cross Plains, Texas memorialized the eccentric author with a museum and a Barbarian Day in September. Vincent d'Onofrio played Howard in the movie, *The Whole Wide World* (1996), about the last years of his brief life.

Vincent and Maria Cosumano were my Sicilian-born maternal grandparents. My grandfather approved of my education, but was furious at my conversion. Apparently, religion had left a bad taste. My grandmother, however, is the only family member to have left artifacts of a Catholic religious life: rosary beads, prayer books, and an edition of Dante's *Divine Comedy* illustrated by Albrecht Durer.

John F. Crocker, IV: He stands 6 feet 6 inches tall, was an oarsman and my roommate for 3 years at Harvard. He converted to born-again Christianity in 1971 after a tour in the Army. I was present at the time of his prayer to receive Jesus Christ as his personal Lord and Savior. He was married twice and has an adopted daughter named Melanie. For many years he taught computer science at Wentworth Junior College in Massachusetts. He now works in a Radio Shack store.

Gil Eisenberg: I met Gil when he was a career counselor at the New York City Youth Board, a social service agency. He became my chief *confidant* while I was in England and he earned the doctorate in psychology.

Timothy English led me to Jesus Christ via his use of the Bible and his personal testimony. He had been through some of the worst trips of the '60's – sex, drugs, and satanism. At the time of my salvation, March 1971, he was a graduate student in the Stanford University architecture department.

Art Evans and I served as spares for the Harvard/U.S. crew the summer of 1967. We were team alternates at the Canadian Nationals at St. Catherine's, Ontario, the Pan American Games in Winnipeg, Canada and the European Championships in Vichy, France. Art became the stroke of the U.S. eight at the Mexico City Olympics.

Volney Foster chaired the Porcellian Club as an undergraduate. Contrary to the tale here, he became not a stockbroker but an agent for classical musicians in New York City.

Ian H. Gardiner rowed on three undefeated Harvard Heavyweight crews 1965-1967. 1967 he stroked the Harvard/U.S. eight for the Pan American Games (1st place) and the European Rowing Championships (2nd place). After the Army and Harvard Business School, he became a securities dealer in Boston. He was one of my best friends at Harvard. He chairs the Friends of Harvard Rowing. His daughter and son are married.

John H. Gardiner, Ian's father, was a creative real estate man and generous supporter of Harvard rowing. He was instrumental in getting me into the Porcellian Club and giving me many enjoyable memories of Boston.

Josie Gardiner, whom Ian married in 1970, now conducts her own aerobics health club. She has raised two children who are married.

Richard (Dick) Grossman was my roommate for 3 years and a Harvard heavyweight crew coxswain. After law school he concluded that rowing would be his life; Dick became a Dartmouth College crew coach and coaches there.

Karen Hawes, a hippie friend introduced to me by Billy Clinton, starred in the Austrian and German productions of *Hair*. We all went to see the Grateful Dead Christmas week 1969 at Fillmore East. She attended the famous New Year's Eve concert of Jimi Hendrix. She and her friend Alan stayed with me in Cambridge. She visited me without Alan at the Stanford boathouse when I was coaching there.

Mudi (Annelise) Hellberg, my Danish girlfriend in England was an expert seamstress. She came from Copenhagen to be an *au pair* and a language student in Cambridge.

James Hervey-Bathurst and I rowed together on the victorious Trinity College clinker four. Previously he had rowed at Eton. At Cambridge he rowed on the Trinity College eight and the University Blue Boat. After Trinity, he and his wife invested great energy reviving his family home and public tourist attraction, Eastnor Castle in Herefordshire. They have three teenage daughters. James provided the only photos I could find of Mudi. His wife, Sarah, writes a column for the British *Country Life* magazine.

Paul Hoffman was Harvard heavyweight crew coxswain *extraordinaire* 1965-1968. He is in the Harvard Athletic Hall of Fame with the oarsmen of our era. He attended Harvard Law School and now practices law in St. Thomas, Virgin Islands. He has a wife and one daughter.

Tom Ireland has been a friend since the 7th grade at Horace Mann. Later he became a roommate and Harvard Lightweight oarsman. He wrote the best senior thesis in the Modern Languages department on Joseph Conrad. He was a *confidant* in letters while I was in England. He lives in New Mexico, and writes novels.

Joe Kanon, roommate for my second year at Cambridge, was Executive Vice President of Houghton Mifflin. Currently, he is best-selling author of three mystery novels: *Los Alamos*, *The Prodigal Spy*, and *The Good German*. He lives in Manhattan with his wife and two sons.

Veronique Kantor showed me hospitality in Paris. She opened the door for me to the real Paris of the times. I met her on the docks of Naples. In Paris, she was at home with artists, student protestors and modern writers.

Ken Kesey — college wrestler, best-selling author, and hipster who coined the term "on the bus" from his bus ride cross-country with the Merry Pranksters and a huge cache of LSD. Eventually, Tom Wolfe's account of him in *The Electric Kool-Aid Acid Test* created a similar wanderlust in me. He died in 2001.

John S. Knight, III was a Harvard roommate of John McKinnon. After Harvard he attended Oxford. He said of Mudi, "She is the most beautiful girl in the world. She literally stops traffic." McKinnon, Knight and I travelled to Marrakesh together, spring 1969. As heir of the Knight-Ridder publications, he was a reporter for the *Philadelphia Inquirer* when he was stabbed to death in his apartment overlooking Ritten House Square, December 7, 1975, the year I entered Westminster Theological Seminary. John and Rosemary McKinnon were chief witnesses at the trial of his murderers.

Andrew Larkin occupies a secure position in Harvard's rowing pantheon as the strong six-man from the Harvard crews of 1966-1968. Tiff Wood, a subject of David Halberstam's *The Amateurs*, said "I know Andy, he's a god." We traveled to California in his MGB the summer of 1970. Andy is the fourth generation M.D. of his family.

Irene Lindon: I met the sad, sweet friend of Veronique Kantor on the docks of Naples the summer of 1968. Her father, the editor of Midnuit Press, published Beckett in Paris.

Cleve Livingston was the bowman of what would become the most famous Harvard crews: — The 1967 Pan American Team (all Harvard), The 1968 U.S. Olympic eight (all Harvard), and The 1972 U.S. Olympic eight (almost all Harvard). Cleve opened his home to me in Sacramento, 1970, when I was morbidly immersed in Conan stories and occultism. From there I got the job as Stanford freshman crew coach. He is married, has two sons and practices law.

Mike Livingston, the younger brother of Cleve, also was an Olympic oarsman. Like his brother, he is in the Harvard Hall-of-Fame and an attorney. He played the violin. The two Livingston brothers and the two Hobbs brothers would drive the U.S. Rowing Team in the era. He lives in Hawaii with his family.

Charles Manson was the utter dark side of the hippie culture. An occultist, he reputedly had ties to the Crowley group, *Ordo Templis Orientalis* (OTO). I visited Christians at the Vacaville State Prison around 1974 when both Timothy Leary and Manson were incarcerated there.

John McKinnon was a close friend for both the Harvard and Cambridge years. He rowed and was a superb scholar. We shared parallel fellowships at Cambridge. His took him to Emmanuel College, mine to Trinity College. He practices psychiatry in Montana and started a camp for troubled adolescents with his wife.

Rosemary Fletcher McKinnon is the daughter of a British diplomat, Cambridge graduate and mother of three daughters. She is the social worker for the camp that she and John run for troubled adolescents.

Myron Miller was a brilliant Horace Manner, and host for Ken Frisoff and me as we were applying to Harvard the senior year at Horace Mann. Eventually, an architect and movie producer of Chaim Potok's novel, *The Chosen*.

Linda Muller: If natural goodness can get you into heaven, then she's in. She and her twin sister, Susan, topped the classes at P.S. 6, New York's Lenox High School and Wellesley College. Linda also did an M.A. in Modern French at Columbia University. She was an inspiration to me, as I was close to her for at least fourteen years of education. Head of the English department at Connecticut's Greenwich Academy, she is a distant cousin of Albert Einstein. She rows for a master's eight. She is married and has two adult daughters.

Shawn Murphy was a Wellesley classmate of Linda Muller. She and I dated briefly our freshman years.

Giles Musson was a brilliant, radical hipster of Trinity College. He led us on romps that seemed to come out of the mind of Bacchus or R. Crumb. He became a banker and died in 1997.

Harry L. Parker: Soft-spoken coach, he is still on the river with Harvard. He holds the title for most collegiate wins in American crew. I rowed for him at the beginning of his dynasty. His personality has attracted a lot of ink, since he is variously described as enigmatic and mysterious. He may simply have a clue to the young man's soul: "boys just want to have fun." Probably, he wishes his personality had attracted less ink and more income. He is the father of two sons and one daughter.

Peta Penson: My first serious girlfriend at Harvard. She obtained the Ph.D. in English. She raised a family, taught and is married to classmate Dr. Peter Banys.

William Quinn: Before becoming Horace Mann's football and wrestling coach, he played on HM's football team with Jack Kerouac. He was one of Boston College's famous "Flying Four." Now retired from coaching at Horace Mann, he lives in Arizona.

Thomas Reilly was head of the Language Department at Horace Mann. He introduced Russian studies at the secondary level in the U.S. Fluent in a dozen different languages, he retired in 1995.

Pat Rensma: I met her in the caves of Matala. She was with her Great Dane Cerberus. She was a Ph.D. candidate in philosophy at the University of Pennsylvania. She visited me in New York the summer of 1970.

Frank Ritter was my best friend at Horace Mann. He was quarterback for the football team and played basketball. In the spring, he was pitcher and switch hitter for the baseball team. We traveled cross-country the summer of 1965. His father arranged for us to be wined and dined in Las Vegas and the Bahamas. A businessman, he resides in Long Island and is the father of two sons.

Dave Roper was my first pastor. He used to walk the circumference of Stanford University, praying for the students. He saw terrific responses to the gospel in the 1960's and 1970's. He and wife Caroline were the first to encourage me to study New Testament Greek, and gave me financial support. He currently pastors, counsels and writes in Boise, Idaho.

Roderick "Hans" Sigward (Siegwardt): My father hailed from Frankfurt, Germany. He was a physical education teacher. He owned a gymnasium in midtown New York. He died at age 60, June 1966.

Angela Sigward: My mother was born in Brooklyn, New York in 1908 of Sicilian parents. Although Sicilian was her first language, she eventually earned a B.A. and three M.A.'s. She was a social worker among the poor and disadvantaged. She died January 7, 2002.

Ellen Sigward was my sister. She attended Hunter High School and Bennington College. She wanted to be an actress, but died of cancer at age 42 in 1985.

Stan Thomas: Horace Mann's outstanding athlete and citizen while I was there. One day I saw him run through the line — directing the traffic of blockers, throwing huge hip fakes, outrunning the secondary. He astounded the city of his day with breath-taking gallops in football. He influenced my own high school desires and dreams. He attended Yale and died fairly young a few years ago. He ran through our hearts, and with his early death, he ran beyond us, and left us wanting more.

Tom Tiffany: Harvard coxswain from the Golden Age of Harvard crew, we traveled to California in 1970 where we climbed mountains and tried to fathom life. He coached MIT crew. He lives and works in Cambridge, Massachusetts.

Andrew Tobias was a classmate at Horace Mann and Harvard. He popularized the Harvard *Let's Go* Series of travel books while a student. At 23, he was the youngest CEO in America. Author of numerous books on finance, he was the Finance Chairman of the 2000 Democratic Presidential campaign.

Cornelius Van Til (1895-1987): One of the original professors at Westminster Theological Seminary, where he taught apologetics 1929-1972. I took his last class, "The Theology of Karl Barth," 1975 while he was an emeritus professor. He influenced generations of students to be Reformed in thought and life. Uniting Reformed theology and apologetics he earned the title, "Father of Presuppositional Apologetics." He thought C. S. Lewis, while a brilliant literary man, taught a truncated Christianity, "an inkling of theology," he would say.

Ted Washburn began coaching the Harvard freshman crew in 1965, my own first year at Harvard. He and Harry Parker would create a dynasty of victorious crews based upon novel approaches to training and equipment.

Tom Wolfe began writing about various hip scenes in the 1960's for *The New York Herald Tribune. The Electric Kool-Aid Acid Test* was his first full-length book. Best known for *Bonfire of the Vanities*, he continues to write. In 2002 he spoke at memorials for Ken Kesey.

Fred Wood was a hitchhiker I picked up outside of Redwood City who told me an extraordinary story about being thrown overboard from his sailboat and being rescued from drowning by praying to God. He began my search of the Scriptures. He drove the coach's launch for spring training of the Stanford freshmen crew.

OTHER WORKS BY ERIC SIGWARD

When Tragedy Strikes

The Works of Cornelius Van Til, 1895-1987 CD-ROM

To purchase additional copies of this book visit:
http://www.ericsigward.com.